Politics, War, and Personality

Fifty Iconic World War II Documents That Changed the World

I would say to the House, as I said to those

who have joined this Government: "I have nothing

to offer you but blood, toil, tears and sweat."

Winston S. Churchill

— Spoken on May 13, 1940 in first address as
Prime Minister before the House of Commons

Politics, War, and Personality

Fifty Iconic World War II Documents That Changed the World

All documents are originals and exhibited at the Museum of World War II, Boston.

"The museum is the repository for the actual
Holy Grail documents of World War II."
—Tom Hanks

Kenneth W. Rendell

Foreword by John S.D. Eisenhower

www.whitman.com

Politics, War, and Personality

Fifty Iconic World War II Documents That Changed the World

© 2013 Whitman Publishing, LLC

3101 Clairmont Rd., Suite G, Atlanta, GA 30329

Correspondence concerning this book may be directed to the publisher, Attn: Politics, War, and Personality, at the address above.

ISBN: 0794839428
Printed in China.

If you enjoy *Politics, War, and Personality: Fifty Iconic World War II Documents That Changed the World*, you will also like *World War II: Saving the Reality* (Rendell); *The Great War: A World War I Historical Collection* (Dalessandro and Mahan); *100 Greatest Military Photographs* (Dalessandro, Mahan, and Morelock); *America's Heroes: Stories From Today's Armed Forces*; and the official U.S. Army in World War II series covering the European Theater: *Chronology: 1941–1945* (Williams); *Cross-Channel Attack* (Harrison); *Breakout and Pursuit* (Blumenson); *The Lorraine Campaign* (Cole); *The Siegfried Line Campaign* (MacDonald); *The Ardennes: Battle of the Bulge* (Cole); *Riviera to the Rhine* (Clarke and Smith); and *The Last Offensive* (MacDonald). For a complete catalog of numismatic and historical reference books, supplies, and storage products, visit Whitman Publishing online at www.Whitman.com.

Scan this QR code to browse Whitman Publishing's full catalog of books.

Contents

Foreword

We are living today in a world in which our capacity to duplicate and create "virtual reality" dominates our lives. That fact makes it doubly refreshing to participate in an area of activity in which authenticity is not only the norm; it is demanded. Nothing in Ken Rendell's Museum of World War II near Boston, Massachusetts, is a copy; every item is authentic, original, and real—so far as a human is able to make it so.

This book, *Politics, War, and Personality: Fifty Iconic World War II Documents That Changed the World,* gives us a fleeting glimpse of the storehouse of historic items that are enshrined in that museum. Though it includes only 50 of some 8,000 documents and artifacts, it represents a sampling of what a visitor might see there. Therein, perhaps, lies the book's main purpose: a menu to tempt the person with a sense of history to make a pilgrimage to the Boston area to view the greatest collection of World War II items in the country.

Most of us, of course, will never be afforded the chance to visit the museum in person. The 50 documents, therefore, stand on their own, reproducing the flavor of the museum itself.

For me, *Politics, War, and Personality* has performed an interesting function, that of restoring perspective. Having been born shortly after the end of World War I, almost concurrently with the first of this book's documents, I personally recall a good many of the events covered by these documents when they happened. Walking down the streets of Denver when Adolf Hitler seized power in Germany is a vivid memory (I was 11). I lived four years in the Philippines, always conscious of the Japanese menace. In the summer of 1938, my father and I, standing in the halls of Fitzsimmons Army Hospital, indulged in a long, sobering discussion of the notorious Munich Agreement, which had just been signed.

As time went on, however, my world began to focus on the European area. Circumstances made that inevitable. In 1942 my father became the Allied Commander for the invasion of North Africa, later Supreme Commander in Europe. As a lieutenant, I served in Germany during the last weeks of the war against Hitler. A great deal of my writing career has centered around the war in the Mediterranean and Northern Europe. As a result, I unwittingly tended to equate Europe with the entire war.

Perusing the documents in this book has, I think, restored much of my perspective. They have reminded me how vast the war was, how much transpired in Russia, the Pacific, and the Far East. Much happened besides Operation Overlord, important though it was. I know that *Politics, War, and Personality* will do the same for others.

Ken Rendell, master collector, literary sleuth, and historian, has given us a book that I will long treasure and restudy. Thousands of others will do the same.

John S.D. Eisenhower

John S.D. Eisenhower is a retired Brigadier General, World War II veteran, and military historian. He has written numerous books, including The Bitter Woods, *a critically acclaimed study of the Battle of the Bulge. He is the son of President Dwight D. Eisenhower.*

Nothing gives a closer intimacy with the people and events of history than the actual documents that mark momentous events and the original letters discussing turning points—political, military, and personal.

Handwriting says a great deal about people, but it also signifies much about the circumstances when it was written. Franklin Roosevelt's bold *OK* and *FDR* on his June 18, 1940, message (number 11), compared to his signature five years later (number 42), show the ravages of the war on him. Adolf Hitler's signature when making his proposal that England and Germany collaborate on the "reestablishment of a natural European balance of power" shows all of the confidence of someone making such a proposal (number 5). The day after the sudden death of one of his top officials, Hitler's signature is very cramped (number 22). Paul von Hindenburg's order (number 6) dissolving the Reichstag is signed with all the importance of this document.

Dwight Eisenhower's great ability to maintain an even disposition while dealing with the personalities of Churchill, Montgomery, de Gaulle, Roosevelt, and the hundreds of others on the Allied side, as well as the Germans, is seen in the consistency of his signatures throughout this book (numbers 23, 28, 31, 33). Similarly, Winston Churchill's handwriting, whether on his almost hourly messages to France during the dark days of the Battle of France (numbers 8, 9, 10) or in October 1944, when the end of the war was in sight (number 30), is unaffected.

Perhaps more than any other document, the draft of the Munich Agreement (number 7) shows this. The British Ambassador's notes for Prime Minister Chamberlain are small and cramped, while Hitler's changes are large and bold—illustrating their mutual positions.

Original letters can show an unexpected side of historical personalities. Erwin Rommel writing to his wife *(Dearest Lu)* and Dwight Eisenhower to his wife *(My Darling)* both (number 33) show great affection, on the same day (June 9, 1944), with very different forecasts for the future.

Dwight Eisenhower's letters to his wife, Mamie, show a very personal and affectionate side of him that most would not expect from the Commander-in-Chief in wartime. Ike frequently expressed his great longing for Mamie, and his dreams of their future together after the war.

A contrasting side to the strongman dictators of the war can be seen in their letters. Benito Mussolini in 1908 (number 3) trying to get away from his debt-ridden and unemployed life; Adolf Hitler in prison in 1924 (number 2) withdrawing from public politics; and Hideki Tojo in prison in 1945 as a war criminal (number 48) demanding his religious and family rights.

The letters of some leaders show the personality one expects—Churchill is always full of force in his letters and George Patton is always George Patton, whether telling his father as a new cadet at West Point (number 19) that he hopes wars will continue, or the Sultan of Morocco (number 20) that he will destroy his country with the utmost violence known to man, or promising, during the Battle of the Bulge (number 37), that the Germans will be much less numerous when he gets through with them.

Dwight Eisenhower wrote two of the most amazing letters of the war. His letter (number 23) on February 15, 1943, detailing to his wife the stress of being Commander-in-Chief with no one to pass decisions to, nor confidants (only his pillow and only the underside of that), and that all his mistakes are expressed in loss of life or disaster for the nation, is the finest statement of the responsibilities of command.

Eisenhower's humanity is expressed in many of his letters but in none more so than his letter of April 16, 1944 (number 31). Three weeks before D-Day and two years after he arrived in Europe as commanding general for the European Theatre, he writes:

How I wish this cruel business of war could be completed quickly. . . . It is a terribly sad business to tot up the casualties each day—even in an air war—and to realize how many youngsters are gone forever. A man must develop a veneer of callousness that lets him consider such things dispassionately, but he can never escape a recognition of the fact that back home the news brings anguish and suffering to families all over the country. Mothers, fathers, brothers, sisters, wives and friends must have a difficult time preserving any comforting philosophy and retaining any belief in the eternal righteousness of things. War demands great toughness of fibre—not only in the soldier that must endure, but in the home that must sacrifice their best.

No one was ever more articulate about what war is all about.

Kenneth W. Rendell
Founder and Director
Museum of World War II

The Museum of World War II uniquely integrates the human story with the political and military issues and events that were transpiring in all the countries and cultures leading up to and during the world at war. The objects, artifacts, letters, and documents in the exhibitions offer insight into the information, influences, and events on both the home fronts and the war fronts. They are what people saw, what they read, and what they used; from the tiniest of spy gadgets to an original landing craft, from guns concealed in a cigarette to an all-original Sherman tank, from the lightness of propaganda leaflets to the huge gold swastika used on Hitler's speaker's stand in Nürnberg. From the beauty of many of the Allies' posters, to the horror of the Holocaust, it is all represented in the museum, with a minimum of signage and no political correctness. The museum is about the ordinary people who made up the social movements and the combatants in the war. But it is also about the leaders, with the most important letters, documents, and artifacts of those who led their countries politically and militarily. The anxiety people felt can never be conveyed, but the influences, lives, and decision-making that changed the world are shown in a more comprehensive way than in any other museum.

The museum's website is www.MuseumofWorldWarII.org.

Hitler's Anti-Semitic Rant Handwritten on the Announcement of the Versailles Treaty
June 28, 1919

This broadside announcement of the signing of the Versailles Peace Treaty, imposed on Germany at the end of World War I, was issued by the Munich *Neueste Nachrichten* newspaper. Hitler wrote his reaction in the lower right, drawing on a well of hatred for the situation Germany found herself in at the end of the Great War. Anti-Semitism was a part of European life in the early 1900s, but seemed to be fading as countries prospered and people did not need to find a scapegoat for their economic ills.

The Versailles Treaty's draconian terms were dictated by France in retaliation for being defeated by Germany in the Franco-Prussian War of 1870. Hitler hated the humiliation the treaty brought upon Germany, particularly the declaration of German guilt.

THIS STATEMENT BY HITLER MAY BE HIS EARLIEST KNOWN ATTACK ON THE JEWS. Hitler did not attack the Jews verbally until two months later. This broadside was recently discovered folded up and saved by Hitler in a file cabinet in his Munich apartment, and is now in the Museum of World War II. In his will, Hitler left the contents of his apartment to his housekeeper. In the same file drawer, he saved newspapers chronicling the victory of the Freikorps over the Bolshevists in Munich, a victory he cheered; two months later came the signing of the Versailles Treaty, which he considered the worst humiliation Germany could suffer.

> *"The peace treaty aims at preparing Germany for the Jewish dictate, the Versailles peace treaty makes the objective of Judah—the destruction of Germany—possible. The Jews must therefore leave Germany."*

Adolf Hitler, handwritten note on printed flier, June 28, 1919.

The Original Program of the Nazi Party
February 24, 1920

Adolf Hitler, printed document, February 24, 1920.

Adolf Hitler attended a meeting of the German Workers Party when it was founded in 1919 and had taken it over by the following year. He formulated the 25-point program that would become the permanent basis of the Nazi Party and published it, as seen here, on February 24, 1920.

The platform of the German Workers Party is a temporary platform. The leaders are against devising new goals once those . . . have been attained for the sole purpose of enabling the Party to go on existing by artificially inciting discontent of the masses.

1. We demand the unification of all Germans . . . to form a Greater Germany.
2. We demand . . . nullification of the Peace Treaties of Versailles.
3. We demand land to feed our people and for the settlements for our population. . . .
4. Only members of our people can be citizens of the State . . . only German blood . . . no Jew can be a member of the people.
7. It is not possible to feed the entire populace, those belonging to foreign nations . . . are to be expended from the Reich.
8. Any further immigration of non-Germans is to be prevented. We demand that all non-Germans who immigrated to Germany since August 2, 1914, be forced to leave the Reich immediately.
10. The activity of the individual may not violate the interests of the general public, but must be within the scope of the whole and to the benefit of all.
11. Abolition of income without work or effort. BREAKING INTEREST SERVITUDE . . . the personal accumulation of wealth through war must be deemed a crime against the people. Therefore we demand the confiscation of all war profits without exception.
13. We demand the nationalization of all businesses (trusts) that have already gone public.

> *"We demand . . . nullification of the Peace Treaties of Versailles. . . . Only members of our people can be citizens . . . only . . . German blood. . . . No Jew can be a member of the people. We demand a share in the profits of large businesses."*

14. We demand a share in the profits of large businesses.
17. We demand . . . the passage of a law for taking land for the welfare of the public without compensation. Abolition of land rental and the prevention of land speculation.
18. Common criminals against the people . . . to be penalized with death. . . .
20. The acquiring of the idea of the State must be attained at the beginning of comprehension through the schools (civics instruction).
22. We demand the formation of a people's army.
23. To enable the establishment of a German press, we demand that a) all editors-in-chief and staffers of newspapers published in German be members of the people, b) non-German newspapers require the express permission of the State for publication . . . newspapers which act contrary to the common weal are to be banned. We demand laws against a tendency in art and literature which has a corrupting influence on the life of our people, and . . . PUBLIC GOOD BEFORE SELF-INTEREST.

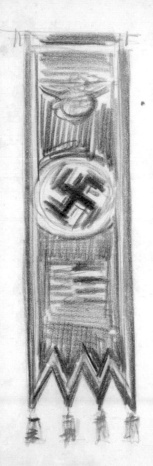

Adolf Hitler's sketch of the Nazi banner.

The Chaos in the Nazi Party
With Hitler in Prison for Treason
for the Munich Beer Hall Putsch
June 16, 1924

> *"I have . . . decided to withdraw from all public politics until I regain my freedom which will once again give me the possibility of complete leadership. I must therefore declare to you that as of now no one has the right to act in my name, claim my authorization, or issue declarations in my name. Similarly, from now on I ask you to desist from sending me letters with political content."*

Adolf Hitler looks out the window of his Landsberg Prison cell.

Adolf Hitler took over the recently formed German Workers Party in 1920, renaming it the National Socialist German Workers Party. In 1923, it was a predominantly Bavarian movement: Erich Ludendorff, the World War I general and postwar political leader, forced Hitler into an agreement in March 1923 in which the Freedom Party would be dominant in northern Germany and the Nazis in the South. In November 1923, Hitler made an uncharacteristic misjudgment of the situation and staged the Munich Beer Hall Putsch in an attempt to overthrow the Bavarian government. Various members of Hitler's group were wounded, including Hermann Goering, and Hitler was arrested and tried for treason. He was sentenced to five years in prison.

The intrigues that characterized German political and military life at the time were mastered by Hitler, but with his unexpected imprisonment, the combination of his rivals and factionalism put the Nazi Party into chaos. Hitler had held the party firmly together, but even with the great freedom allowed him in Landsberg Prison (Rudolf Hess had voluntarily accompanied him as his secretary), the Party was leaderless at a critical time. Competing individuals and groups were asserting Hitler's authority and backing, while his core of supporters was being marginalized.

In this letter Hitler writes from his prison cell about the intrigues with Ludendorff and the rival Freedom Party, stating that "I now see . . . that many local and individual associations are totally opposed to a merger with the Freedom Party. . . . I have learned of the expulsion of a number of old Party comrades from the movement by bodies whose makeup is unclear to me. Under such circumstances it is no longer possible for me to intervene somehow from now on, or indeed to assume any responsibility.

"I have therefore decided to withdraw from all public politics until I regain my freedom, which will once again give me the possibility of complete leadership. I must therefore declare to you that as of now no one has the right to ask in my name, claim my authorization, or issue declarations in my name. Similarly, from now on I ask you to desist from sending me letters with political content."

Hitler was released on parole in December 1924, by which time the Nazi Party had lost significant popular support and was on the extreme fringe of the political spectrum in Germany.

Landsberg den 16. Juni 1924.

abgesandt 24.6.24

Herrn Haase
Göttingen
Obere Karspüle 17 a I.

Sehr geehrter Herr!

Ich erhalte soeben Ihr Schreiben vom 14. Juni
das ich auch hiermit gleich beantworte.

Ich muß zuerst eine kleine Richtigstellung
vornehmen. Es ist nicht richtig, daß ich gegenüber den
Herren der Landesverbände eine Verschmelzung der beiden
Parteien als solche etwa grundsätzlich abgelehnt habe.
Ich teilte damals den Herren mit, daß durch die Partei
in Thüringen an mich das Ansinnen nach Vereinigung
gerichtet wurde; daß ich darauf hin Exllz. L. die
Angelegenheit vortrug mit dem Bemerken / persönlich
dann einverstanden zu sein, wenn die Voraussetzungen
hiefür gegeben seien. Diese Voraussetzungen mußten in
meinen Augen doppelte sein: erstens in Bezug auf die
ideelle Leitung, zweitens durch Gründung einer einheit-
lichen Organisation. Um diese Voraussetzungen zu erhalten
bat ich um eine sofortige Besprechung mit Herrn v. Gräefe.

Herr von G. kam zunächst nicht , statt dessen wurde
eine Erklärung veröffentlicht , die ich , da nach meiner
Meinung von damals , Herr v. G. I ihr Verfasser und Urheber
war , für illoyal halten mußte. Dies war allerdings ein Ir-
tum , insoferne die Erklärung durch Exllz. L. veranlaßt
war , in dem Glauben, die zwischenHerrn v. Gräefe und mir
noch stattfindende Besprechung werde ein günstiges
Ergebniß haben. /Diese Zusammenkunft fand auch statt,
jedoch mit negativem Resultat. Herr v. G. teilte mir
dabei die bereits erfolgte Veröffentlichung nicht mit.

Exllz. L. der die Sache nun aufklärte , veranlaßte
eine neue Zusammenkunft, in der Hoffnung diesesmal zu
einer möglichen Grundlage kommen zu können. Tatsächlich
wurden besonders von Exllz. L. meine Forderungen als
zu mindest theoretisch richtig anerkannt und auch von
Ihm persönlich auf das wärmste vertreten. Auch Herr v.G.
änderte seinen Standpunkt in so wesentlichen Punkten,
daß sich in der Folge eine nicht schädliche Verschmelzung
ergeben könnte. Da die Verhandlungen nicht abgeschlossen
wurden, bat mich Herr v. G. zu veranlassen daß nicht in
der Zwischenzeit durch gegenseitigen Kampf die weiteren
Verhandlungen zerschlagen würden. Ich unterschrieb
einen kurzen Aufruf in diesem Sinne.

Dies ist der Hergang der Sache.

--2--

Wie ich nun aus einer ganzen Reihe von Zuschriften
und Kundgebungen ersehe , lehnen zahlreiche Ortsgruppen
und einzelne Verbäde das Zusammengehen mit der Freiheits-
partei grundsätzlich ab.

Endlich erfahre ich vom Ausschluß einer Anzahl alter
Parteigenossen aus der Bewegung, durch Tagungen deren
Zusammensetzung mir unklar ist. Es ist mir unter solchen
Verhältnissen nicht mehr möglich von hier aus irgendwie
einzugreifen , oder gar eine Verantwortung zu übernehmen.

Ich habe deshalb beschlossen, mich auf solange von der
ganzen öffentlichen Politik zurückzuziehen, bis mir
die wiedergegebene Freiheit auch die Möglichkeit eines
tatsächlichen Führens XXXXX bietet.

Ich muß Ihnen deshalb erklären, daß ab jetzt niemand
mehr das Recht besitzt in meinem Namen zu handeln, sich
auf mich zu berufen, oder in meinem Namen Erklärungen
abzugeben.

Ebenso bitte ich von jetzt ab keine Briefe politischen
Inhalts mehr an mich zu richten.

Mit treudeutschem Heilgruß

Ihr Ihnen persönlich und den anderen Herren herzlich
ergebener

Adolf Hitler

Adolf Hitler, typewritten and signed letter, June 16, 1924.

|||

A Debt-Ridden and Unemployed Mussolini Confronts His Future
1908

"Life in this semi-wild village of my birth is beginning to weigh on me, and to get away from it I got an idea...."

Benito Mussolini, Il Duce, future Fascist dictator of Italy, wrote from the town of his birth, Predappio, in 1908:

You know that I have been granted the right to teach French and that I also know German very well, so that there would be no difficulty in teaching it. But up to now I haven't found a way to keep busy. In truth, I haven't been privy to great ideas due to the domestic business. But life in this semi-wild village of my birth is beginning to weigh on me, and to get away from it I got an idea some time ago. I'll explain it to you now because I need your advice. I have in mind coming to Siena as a private tutor of modern languages. You are in a position to tell me if "I can sell my product" and can assist me. Next July I will be taking my high-school-teacher's exams, and if I pass, as I hope I will, I will enroll in law school.

Benito Mussolini.

In 1904, Mussolini had left Switzerland, where he had been a schoolmaster. His teaching contract had not been renewed, his next job as a bricklayer was unsatisfactory, and his subsequent imprisonment for vagrancy was distasteful. Back in Italy, as his biographer notes, Mussolini was "a private soldier in a rifle-regiment famed for its jog-trot pace and the green cock's feather plumes drooping from round tilted hats. From 1906 to 1907, he was . . . an impecunious (£2 a month) second-grade teacher at a mountain town . . . noted as a master who kept chaos from his classroom only through bribery. Powerless to control his forty-strong class of urchins, he furtively began the day's lesson by doling out sweets from a paper bag" (Richard Collier, *Duce!*). Then in March 1908, after he received his license to teach French, he again became a schoolmaster. A year later he was working for a Socialist newspaper in Trent; four years later he was editor of *Avanti!*, the leading Socialist paper in Italy. By 1922, he was Prime Minister of Italy.

Carissimo amico,

non ho ricevuto ancora notizia alcuna dal Monte di Paschi circa la domanda che ho avanzato per un mutuo ipotecario.

Sono scivolato, o meglio, siamo scivolati in una crisi pericolosa e l'operazione col Monte de' Paschi è fatta allo scopo di liberarmi dai molteplici impegni a lunga e breve scadenza, coll'unificazione del passivo.

Il qual passivo del resto non ammonta che a un terzo del capitale o poco più.

Piuttosto, il tempo stringe. L'avvocato Ciani di Roux S.C. che iniziò le pratiche, mi assicurava che l'affare avrebbe potuto stabilirsi in

e puoi aiutarmi. Una decina di lezioni settimanali, mi basterebbero al principio, tanto più che verrei fornito di denaro. Aggiungi che al prossimo luglio darò l'esame di licenza liceale e se mi riesce, come lo spero, m'inscriverò in una facoltà di legge, magari anche a Siena.

La prima parte di questo piano ti sembra effettuabile? Dammi una risposta.

Giorni fa mi accadde di pensare a quel tal banchiere senese fallito che ricoverai una notte a Losanna e che tu accompagnasti sino a Fiume. È morto o vivo? E di Annemasse hai saputo più nulla?

Ti saluto caramente e aspetto. Tuo

Mussolini Benito

Benito Mussolini, handwritten and signed letter, 1908.

IV

A Desperate and Wounded Hermann Goering, With Adolf Hitler in Prison, Goes to Italy to Plead With Mussolini for Money to Keep the Fascist Movement Alive in Germany
November 28, 1924

Hermann Goering, later Hitler's head of the Luftwaffe, writes from Venice on November 28, 1924, to Mussolini's agent Leo Negrelli:

You have no idea how right now, before the elections, the democratic and, which is the same thing, Jewish newspapers in Germany are ranting and raving against Fascism and Mussolini, in particular, to make the German voters see that nationalism doesn't know how to govern and particularly that Fascist methods are soon at an end. In accordance with our agreement, we met this propaganda with counter-propaganda. We must of course be that much more pained to see that nothing at all is done by the other side to fulfill our modest wish. We place such high value in the fulfillment of this request because we would then see that the other side is really in earnest in its promises and its friendship for us. But until now only we have really kept the bargain fully, and in doing so we have had a lot of trouble, while the other side has only made promises. Thus, I ask you to write to Rome and depict the situation as it is right now, so that something is finally done by them. Otherwise it shall be very difficult for me to continue making propaganda for Fascism. Also, the matter is urgent for other reasons!!!!!!! I thank you in advance for all your efforts.

VENEDIG 28. XI. 1924.

Lieber Herr Negrelli!

Mit aufrichtiger Freude haben wir die Nachricht von der Geburt Eines Töchterchens erhalten. Wir sandten Ihnen zusammen mit Walthers ein Glückwunschtelegramm. Heute nun wollen wir unsere Wünsche nocheinmal brieflich wiederholen. Wir wünschen der Kleinen eine recht sonnige Zukunft und den Eltern recht viel Freude! Hoffentlich geht es Mutter und Kind jetzt gut und können Sie d s Glück, Vater geworden zu sein ordentlich geniessen.

Nun trotz allen Urlaubs noch ein wenig Politik! Sie ahnen nicht, wie sehr gerade jetzt vor den Wahlen in Deutschland von jüdischen und demokratischen, was ja dasselbe ist, Zeitungen gegen den Fascismus und ganz besonders Mussolini gehetzt wird, damit die deutschen Wähler sehen sollen, dass der Nationalismus nicht zu regieren versteht und besonders fscistische Methoden schnell ausrangiert sind. Gegen diese Propaganda haben wir nun eine Gegenpropaganda ausgeführt, gemäss unseren Abmachungen. Umso schmerzlicher müssen wir es natürlich empfinden, wenn wir sehen, dass von der anderen Seite so garnichts gemacht wird, um unseren gewiss bescheidenen Wunsch zu erfüllen. Wir legen deshalb so grossen Wert auf die ERfüllung dieser Bitte, weil wir daraus erseheen würden, dass es der Gegenseite wirklich auch Ernst ist mit Ihren Zusagen und einer Freundschaft mit uns. Aber bis heute haben wirklich nur wir unsere Zusagen voll gehalten und deshalb auch viel Unanehmlichkeiten gehabt, Während die Gegenseite nur Versprechungen gemacht hat. Ich bitte Sie deshalb nach Rom zu schreiben und die Lage, wie sie derzeit ist, schildern,damit von dort endlich etwas getan wird. Da es sonst für mich sehr schwer ist, weiterhin Propaganda für den Fascismus zu treiben. Auch aus anderen Gründen eilt die Sache!!!!!!! Ich danke Ihnen im voraus für alle Bemühungen und bin mit den besten Grüssen von mir und meiner Frau an Sie Beide Ihr ergebener *Hermann Göring*

Hermann Goering, typewritten and signed letter, November 28, 1924.

Throughout the 1920s Hitler's National Socialist Party was a predominantly Bavarian movement. The future German dictator prematurely played his hand in November 1923, staging the Munich Beer Hall Putsch, which was calculated to overthrow the Bavarian government. The plan backfired; Hitler and several of his followers were arrested. The wounded Goering, first aided by a Jewish proprietor (according to William Shirer's monumental history *The Rise and Fall of the Third Reich*), then fled to Austria, where he was treated in an Innsbruck hospital.

At this time, Goering

was in a Venice hotel attempting to negotiate a badly needed loan from . . . Mussolini. Although still recuperating from his painful wound, which required heavy drug dosage, the former war ace was exerting himself in the Führer's service. He was involved in a frustrating correspondence with . . . Negrelli, an agent of Mussolini, in hopes of getting two million lire from the Fascists as well as a promise from *Il Duce* to see Hitler once he was out of prison. In return the National Socialists would publicly support Italy's claim to the South Tyrol—an action that would lose numerous supporters, particularly in Bavaria. But apparently the Fascists doubted they would get their money's worth from a party whose attempt to emulate the March on Rome had ended so disastrously, and Goering's pleading became shrill . . . In a few years [the NSDAP] would be in power. He enlarged upon the embarrassment [the Party] would face because of its support of such an unpopular cause as the South Tyrol; and pointed out what a bargain Mussolini was getting for a mere two million lire. . . . But the month of November slipped by with Mussolini still refusing to commit himself . . . and the Führer still in prison.[John Toland, *Adolf Hitler*]

In stark contrast stood the increasingly powerful Mussolini. Summoned in 1922 by King Victor Emanuel III to form a ministry, the Fascist leader undertook immediate governmental reform. The electoral laws were altered so as to insure Fascist control, Mussolini took over a number of ministries himself, and all opposition parties and newspapers were suppressed. While Hitler wrote *Mein Kampf* in prison, Mussolini forged a Fascist totalitarian regime to be reckoned with.

Hermann Goering (bottom left) in front of Adolf Hitler, Nürnberg Rally, 1928.

V

One of the Most Important Adolf Hitler Letters, Declaring His Belief That England and Germany Should Have "the closest political collaboration . . . and the reestablishment of a natural European balance of power."
September 30, 1931

This letter was written on September 30, 1931, to Sefton Delmer, a British newspaper journalist in Berlin who was Hitler's favorite reporter and the only reporter who accompanied Hitler on his campaign airplane.

Greatly as I am honoured by your kind invitation that I should express my views concerning the present crisis in Britain, my misgivings about undertaking this task are no less great. I am afraid part of the British public might consider it presumptuous of me, were I as a German to put forward views in a British newspaper which in conformity with my knowledge and my conscience can only be a criticism of political measures and proceedings, approved up to now by a large part of the British people. I hope, however, that out of this crisis new readiness will grow up in Britain to submit the past twelve years to a reappraisal. I should be happy, if as a result of this [reappraisal] the unhappy war-psychosis could be overcome on such a scale as to permit the realization of the truly cordial relationship between the British and the German peoples so eagerly desired by myself and my movement. For I believe that the crisis now breaking in on us can only be solved by the closest political collaboration of those nations who see in the re-establishment of a natural European balance of power the first precondition to dealing with those great world problems under which Britain too suffers today.

Hitler always believed that England and Germany were natural allies—the English royal family was partly German and, despite World War I, the English upper classes were supportive all through the 1930s of the order and apparent prosperity the Nazis represented. The former King Edward VIII was a great admirer of Adolf Hitler. Hitler's strong belief, expressed in this letter, was behind his decision to stop the attack when he had the British Army surrounded at Dunkirk and allowed their evacuation to England. Had he continued the attack he would have destroyed the British Army and any hope England had of repelling the planned German invasion.

During June and July 1940, it became clear to Hitler that the new British Prime Minister, Winston Churchill, did not represent the opinions of the right-wing English upper classes; consequently, Hitler unleashed his Luftwaffe against England and the Battle of Britain began. Rudolf Hess still believed, as Hitler had, that war with England didn't make sense, and he made his historic flight to Scotland, a year later, to negotiate a peace with the United Kingdom.

Adolf Hitler, typewritten and signed letter, September 30, 1931.

VI

The Nazis' Control of Germany Is Assured as President von Hindenburg Gives In to Hitler's Demand to Dissolve the Reichstag and Order New Elections— the Last Election Until After World War II
February 1, 1933

Paul von Hindenburg, as President of Germany, ordered new Parliamentary elections as demanded by Hitler, whom he had appointed Chancellor the day before. The Field Marshal, World War I Chief of Staff, and President of Germany since 1925, believed he could control the "Bohemian Corporal" by making him Chancellor. Adolf Hitler was not a politician to be taken lightly; at this time the Nazi Party was a minority and Hindenburg had run for reelection in 1932, at age 84, only to block Hitler from gaining national power.

He gave in to Hitler's demand to dissolve the Reichstag (Parliament), and the Nazi Party immediately set out to drive the other parties out of the election. They succeeded in doing so in the election held later in 1933. As soon as they had control of the Reichstag, Hitler announced that there would be no further elections. The aged Hindenburg, in failing health, lived into 1934; upon his death, Hitler's power was complete.

President Paul von Hindenburg, official order, February 1, 1933.

Chancellor Adolf Hitler greets President Paul von Hindenberg, March 1933.

Hindenburg and Hitler at the May 1 celebrations in Berlin, 1933.

VII

The Munich Agreement:
The Document Hitler and Chamberlain Fought Over, With Hitler's Bold Changes and Chamberlain's Notes.
The Terms Presented by Adolf Hitler for Not Starting World War II
September 23, 1938

The Munich Agreement is generally considered the most important document of World War II. It represents the victory of Adolf Hitler's psychological understanding of the French and the British, and the defeat of the German military's distrust of Hitler's instincts.

This document was Hitler's ultimatum for not starting World War II. In reality, it was the start of the war, because with this agreement Hitler knew that England and France would agree to any terms to prevent another war. The German military, who were ready to overthrow him, also knew that they could trust Hitler's instinct for such a bold move. Europe would never be the same.

This document was Hitler's first statement of his demands to prevent war in 1938. It is the document Hitler presented to British Prime Minister Neville Chamberlain on the night of September 23, 1938. Chamberlain said he couldn't possibly agree to it; they argued furiously, and finally Hitler made the concessions seen here in his bold writing. The much smaller and more finely written notes in English are the British Ambassador's notes to Chamberlain. The boldness of Hitler's writing says everything about the intimacy of this document and the atmosphere at that meeting.

This document, with the changes Hitler made, was agreed to by the British and French and signed in Munich one week later.

The stage was set for Hitler to take over Europe.

Adolf Hitler viewed the existence of Czechoslovakia as one of the outrageous terms of the Treaty of Versailles, which ended World War I and, by its provisions, virtually guaranteed a Second World War.

The Munich Agreement, typed document annotated by Prime Minister Neville Chamberlain and Adolf Hitler, Führer of the German Reich, September 23, 1938.

Adolf Hitler signs the final draft of the Munich Agreement, September 29, 1938.

Among the many nationalities incorporated into Czechoslovakia were 750,000 Sudeten Germans, and, soon after taking power in Germany, the Nazi Party began financing the Sudeten German Party in its demands for more rights. Hitler saw the Sudeten issue as justifying an attack on Czechoslovakia, and after Germany's annexation of Austria in March 1938, it was his primary goal.

England and France, not seeing Hitler's true goal, urged Czechoslovakia to give the Sudeten Germans anything they wanted; but on orders from Hitler, no matter what the Czech government offered, the Sudeten Germans demanded more. Hitler, meanwhile, in May 1938, was preparing for the invasion of Czechoslovakia. He was convinced that France, whose army could theoretically crush Germany, would abandon Czechoslovakia.

Hitler's plans for the attack became known, Czechoslovakia mobilized its army, and Hitler, not yet ready, was forced to back down. Humiliated, on May 28, 1938, he ordered the *Wehrmacht* to be ready to invade Czechoslovakia by October 2 at the latest. Czechoslovakia was to be "wiped off the map."

- 2 -

unter allen Umständen verhindert werden müssen. Es muss eine paritätische Situation geschaffen werden. Das in der anliegenden Karte bezeichnete deutsche Gebiet wird von deutschen Truppen besetzt ohne Rücksicht darauf, ob sich bei der Volksabstimmung vielleicht in diesem oder jenem Teil des Gebiets eine tschechische Mehrheit herausstellt. Andererseits ist das tschechische Gebiet von tschechischen Truppen besetzt ohne Rücksicht darauf, dass innerhalb dieses Gebiets grosse deutsche Sprachinseln liegen, die bei der Volksabstimmung sich ohne Zweifel in der Mehrheit zum deutschen Volkstum bekennen werden.

Zur sofortigen und endgültigen Bereinigung des sudetendeutschen Problems werden daher nunmehr von der Deutschen Regierung folgende ~~Forderungen~~ *Vorschläge gemacht* ~~erhoben~~ :

I.) ~~Sofortige und vollständige~~ Zurückziehung der gesamten tschechischen Wehrmacht, der Polizei, der

Immediate + complete withdrawal of entire Czech armed forces, police + other authorities. Withdrawal to begin Sept. 26 to end by Sept. 29, 8 p.m.

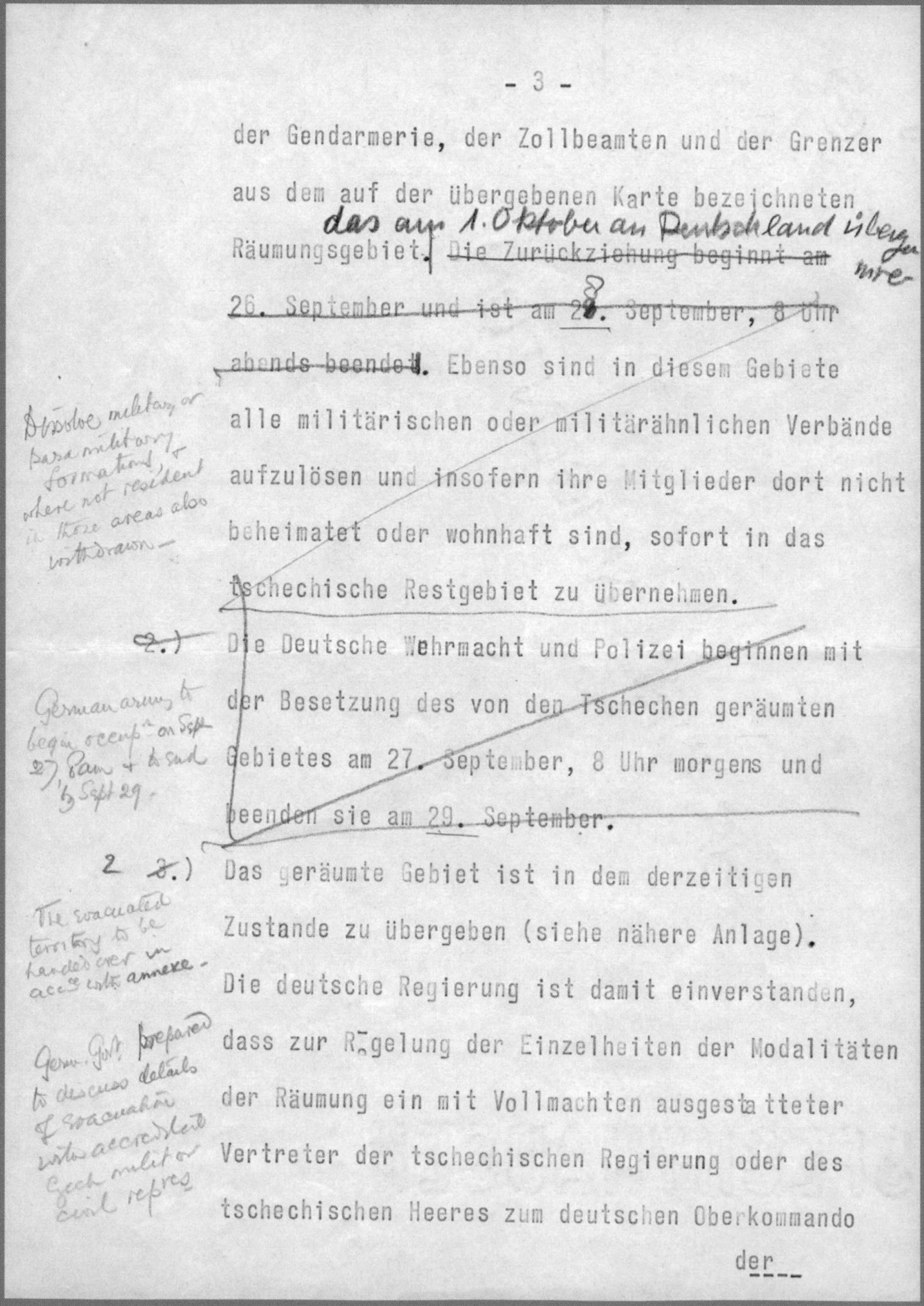

- 3 -

der Gendarmerie, der Zollbeamten und der Grenzer

aus dem auf der übergebenen Karte bezeichneten

das auf 1. Oktober an Deutschland übergeben wre

Räumungsgebiet. ~~Die Zurückziehung beginnt am~~

~~26. September und ist am 29. September, 8 Uhr~~

~~abends beendet.~~ Ebenso sind in diesem Gebiete

alle militärischen oder militärähnlichen Verbände

aufzulösen und insofern ihre Mitglieder dort nicht

beheimatet oder wohnhaft sind, sofort in das

tschechische Restgebiet zu übernehmen.

2.) Die Deutsche Wehrmacht und Polizei beginnen mit

der Besetzung des von den Tschechen geräumten

Gebietes am 27. September, 8 Uhr morgens und

beenden sie am 29. September.

2 3.) Das geräumte Gebiet ist in dem derzeitigen

Zustande zu übergeben (siehe nähere Anlage).

Die deutsche Regierung ist damit einverstanden,

dass zur Regelung der Einzelheiten der Modalitäten

der Räumung ein mit Vollmachten ausgestatteter

Vertreter der tschechischen Regierung oder des

tschechischen Heeres zum deutschen Oberkommando

der

Handwritten margin notes:
- *Dissolve military or paramilitary formations, where not resident in these areas also withdrawn.*
- *German armies to begin occupat'n on Sept 27 8am + to end by Sept 29.*
- *The evacuated territory to be handed over in accord with annexe.*
- *Germ. Gov't prepared to discuss details of evacuation with accredited Czech milit or civil repres.*

Virtually the entire German Army High Command opposed this plan, fearing that if France and England supported Czechoslovakia, their armies would easily overrun Germany from the West while the *Wehrmacht* were fighting the Czechs in the East. The Chief of the Army General Staff, Ludwig Beck, was fired by Hitler in August 1938 for expressing his views that the army should refuse the order to invade Czechoslovakia. During July and August the generals agreed among themselves to overthrow Hitler as soon as he ordered the attack on Czechoslovakia. Their justification would be the overwhelming military superiority of France and England. These countries, England in particular, however, were urging Czechoslovakia to concede whatever was necessary to appease Hitler, and they gave every indication they did not intend to defend Czechoslovakia.

Alarmed at this attitude, General Franz Halder, Beck's successor, sent his emissary on September 2 to directly inform Chamberlain of their plans to overthrow Hitler, and that England and France had to hold firm in their commitment to Czechoslovakia. Chamberlain deferred judgment to his ambassador to Germany, Sir Neville Henderson, who was very supportive of Hitler's demands.

Two days later, an article in the *London Times*, widely believed to convey the government's position, urged Czechoslovakia to cede the Sudetenland to Germany to solve the crisis. The article ignored the fact that this area contained Czechoslovakia's version of the Maginot line and her natural mountain defenses, and would leave her completely defenseless against Nazi Germany.

On September 12, 1938, Hitler, in his closing speech at the Nürnberg Party meeting, demanded justice for the Sudetenland, and on September 15, Chamberlain shocked Hitler by saying that he wanted to come to Germany to solve this issue. Their meeting at Berchtesgaden had predictable results since Hitler sensed that Chamberlain would be willing to cede the Sudetenland.

After the signing (left to right), Chamberlain, French Prime Minister Édouard Daladier, Hitler, and Italian dictator Benito Mussolini pose for a photo.

- 4 -

der Wehrmacht tritt.

3) (4.) Die tschechische Regierung entlässt sofort alle sudetendeutschen Wehrmachts- und Polizei- angehörigen aus dem gesamten tschechischen Staats- gebiet in ihre Heimat.

Czech gov't to release all Sudeten in Czech army

4) (5.) Die tscheshische Regierung entlässt alle wegen politischer Vergehen inhaftierten deutschstämmi- gen Gefangenen.

Release of all Sudeten political prisoners.

5) (6.) Die Deutsche Regierung ist einverstaden, in den näher zu bezeichnenden Gebieten bis spätestens 25. November eine Volksabstimmung stattfinden zu lassen. Die aus dieser Abstimmung sich ergebenden Korrekturen der neuen Grenze werden durch eine *oder eine internationale* deutsch-tschechische Kommission bestimmt. Die Abstimmung selbst findet unter der Kontrolle einer internationalen Kommission statt. Abstimmung: berechtigt sind alle in den in Frage kommenden Gebieten am 28.Oktober 1918 wohnhaften oder bis zum 28.Oktober 1918 dort geborenen Personen. Als Ausdruck des Wunsches zur Zugehörigkeit

Plebiscite on Nov 25

modifications of new frontier by German Czech frontier commi?

Plebiscite itself under control of intert Commin

der

Hitler demanded that Chamberlain cease his threats against Germany, and the British Prime Minister stated that he wasn't threatening Germany. Hitler gave Chamberlain his ultimatum: the Sudeten Germans had to have self-determination, and only if Britain agreed to this would Hitler negotiate further.

During the following week the British cabinet agreed to the cessation, as did the French, and they announced to the Czechs that, treaties notwithstanding, they would not support Czechoslovakia if she refused to give Hitler this part of their country. Initially the Czechs refused, but conceded on September 21—they had no choice.

Chamberlain returned to Germany on September 22, agreeing to everything Hitler had demanded the previous week. Hitler told him these terms were no longer acceptable. He demanded to occupy the Sudetenland within days and expel all Czechs, and that they would be allowed to take no possessions with them. Chamberlain could not agree to Hitler's demands and the meeting broke up. The following day, after an exchange of letters, Hitler and Chamberlain agreed to a final meeting.

At 10:30 p.m. on September 23, Hitler presented Chamberlain with this typewritten statement of his demands. Hitler put his timetable in writing—the Czechs had 48 hours to begin evacuation of the Sudetenland and 96 hours to complete it. With the English Ambassador, Sir Neville Henderson, at this side, making pencil notations on Hitler's memorandum, Chamberlain and Hitler argued furiously over Hitler's demands, which had finally been put in writing. Chamberlain asked if this memorandum was Hitler's final word. Hitler said it was. Chamberlain said he was leaving with his hopes for peace destroyed. Hitler offered a concession—"You are one of the few men for whom I have ever done such a thing." He took the memorandum over

Neville Chamberlain, September 30, 1938: peace in our time?

- 5 -

der Bevölkerung zum Deutschen Reich oder zum
tschechischen Staat gilt die einfache Mehrheit
aller männlichen und weiblichen Abstimmungs-
berechtigten. Zur Abstimmung wird aus den näher
zu bezeichnenden Gebieten auf beiden Seiten das
Militär zurückgezogen. Zeitpunkt und Dauer bestimmen
die deutsche und tschechische Regierung gemeinsam.
6 T.) Zur Regelung aller weiteren Einzelheiten schlägt
die deutsche Regierung die Bildung einer autorisier-
ten deutsch-tschechischen Kommission vor.

Godesberg, den 23. September 1938.

which they had been arguing and changed the date of the occupation of Sudetenland to October 1 and altered some of the phrases Chamberlain would not accept. Chamberlain was overwhelmed by Hitler's gesture, not knowing that October 1 had been Hitler's target date all along.

Chamberlain returned to London on September 24 and tried to persuade his cabinet to accept Hitler's written demands, but this time, they hesitated. The Czechs refused, and the French said they would honor their treaty obligations provided England would back them up. In all the capitols of Europe, war seemed imminent. General Halder and his fellow conspirators prepared to oust Hitler.

During the next four days, Hitler and Chamberlain exchanged letters while Halder brought others into his conspiracy, now set to arrest Hitler on the 28th. Chamberlain began to waver on the British position that there could be no agreement to the September 23 memorandum. The morning of the coup, September 28, Mussolini telephoned to advise Hitler that Chamberlain had asked him to mediate the Czech crisis and avert war. Meanwhile, the French were backing down even further, agreeing to most of the September 23 demands. The coup crumbled as Britain and France agreed to meet with Hitler and Mussolini the next day in Munich.

Mussolini presented his "peace plan," which was eagerly accepted by the British and French. So eager were both delegations to appease Hitler that neither questioned the fact that "Mussolini's proposals" were almost identical to the demands that Hitler had presented to Neville Chamberlain a week earlier—this document—the September 23 memorandum.

The demands of this September 23 document were then agreed to, as the Munich Agreement of September 29. German troops would occupy the Sudetenland on October 1, 1938, as Hitler had planned all along, and as he had demanded on September 23.

Czechoslovakia was the least important of Hitler's games in September 1938. His belief that Britain and France had been so weakened by their experiences of World War I that they would not fight under any circumstances, save direct attack, were proven. At the moment when Hitler could have been defeated militarily by Britain and France, assuming he had survived his own generals' coup, his methods of basing his strategy on his assessment of the Allies' psychological weaknesses were proven correct.

Instead of ending Hitler's rule, the acceptance of this September 23 memorandum emboldened Hitler to trust his instincts even more, undermined the judgment of his generals, and destroyed any further coup attempts for nearly six years—until July 20, 1944—when the war was clearly lost.

VIII

Eleven Days After the German Attack Began, Churchill Tells the President of France How to Fight Against German Tanks
May 21, 1940

"It is not possible to stop columns of tanks from piercing thin lines and penetrating deeply. . . . All ideas of stopping [tanks] . . . are vicious . . . Towns should be held with the riflemen, and tank personnel should be fired upon should they attempt to leave vehicles. . . . Where possible, buildings should be blown down upon them. . . . I feel more confident than I did after the beginning of the battle."

The German army had attacked along the exact same route as they had when they began World War I. France and Britain were convinced in 1914 that it would be impossible for the Germans to attack through the Ardennes, but that is exactly what they did again on May 10, 1940. Churchill had gone to Paris on May 16 to bolster French morale and review the military situation. The night before this letter was written, May 20, the French had appointed a new Commander-in-Chief, Maxime Weygand, in whom Churchill had great confidence, as expressed in this letter.

Within days of Churchill writing this letter, the Germans were driving the French and British armies into the sea at Dunkirk. The French capitulated on June 16, 1940.

Prime Minister Winston Churchill.

G.R.

Not to be shown to anyone else.

Gen. Ismay to see & despatch

F. W. F. 2

Vns.
fr 9/40

General Ismay has seen.

Prime Minister to Monsieur Reynaud.
Personal and Private.

Despatched 21.5.40. Despatch now too.

(*Private*)

Many congratulations upon appointing
Weygand, in whom we have entire confidence here. (Stop)
It is not possible to stop columns of tanks from
piercing thin lines and penetrating deeply. (Stop)
All ideas of stopping holes and hemming in these
intruders are vicious. (Stop)   Principle should be
on the contrary to punch holes.   Undue importance
should not be attached to the arrival of a few tanks at
any particular point. (Stop)   What can they do if
they enter a town. (Stop)   Towns should be held with
riflemen, and tank personnel should be fired upon should
they attempt to leave vehicles. (Stop)   If they cannot
get food or drink or petrol, they can only make a mess
and depart. (Stop)   Where possible, buildings should
be blown down upon them. (Stop)   Every town with
valuable cross-roads should be held in this fashion. (Stop)
Secondly, the tank columns in the open must be hunted
down and attacked in the open country by numbers of small

- 2 -

mobile columns with a few cannon. (Stop)   Their tracks
must be wearing out, and their energy must abate. (Stop)
This is the one way to deal with the armoured intruders.
(Stop)   As for the main body, which does not seem to
be coming on very quickly, the only method is to drive
in upon the flanks. (Stop)   The confusion of this
battle can only be cleared by being aggravated, so that
it becomes a melee. (Stop)   They strike at our communications; we should strike at theirs. (Stop)   I feel more
confident than I did at the beginning of the battle;
but all the Armies must fight at the same time, and I
hope the British will have a chance soon. (Stop)   Above
is only my personal view, and I trust it will give no
offence if I state it to you.   *Every good
wish.*

Winston Churchill

Prime Minister Winston Churchill, typewritten and signed letter, May 21, 1940.

IX

Churchill to the President of France
June 5, 1940

"You have no right to ask us to deprive ourselves of the sole means of continuing the war by casting away in a single battle the already small forces upon which we rely as the sole sure hope of ultimate victory to us both."

"...You don't seem to understand at all [that] the British fighter aviation has been worn to a shred . . . by the need of . . . prolonged standing patrols over Dunkirk without which the evacuation would have been impossible."

The day of this message, which is heavily revised by Churchill and signed with his initials, was the last day Allied soldiers were able to escape from Dunkirk. Germany began the offensive toward Paris. Eleven days later, on June 16, 1940, France capitulated and signed an armistice with Germany.

The French and British armies had been driven back by the shock of the Germans attacking through the Ardennes, effectively going around the French series of fortifications known as the Maginot Line. French leader Charles de Gaulle had correctly written in 1933 that mobile warfare in the future would go around fortifications, not directly attack them. The German commander, Heinz Guderian, wrote in *Achtung-Panzer!* (1937) that the future of warfare would be in mobility; nevertheless, the French and British commanders were prepared to defend France with World War I tactics.

The German Army's *Blitzkrieg* (lightning war) quickly overran France, driving the British and French armies into a pocket around the English Channel town of Dunkirk. Hitler did not drive the Allies into the sea; he slowly tightened the encircling lines, and flotillas of thousands of ships, large and small, evacuated hundreds of thousands of troops to England. The Luftwaffe did diligently strafe the boats, killing thousands, and those left on the beach went into captivity.

6-5

Prime Minister to General Spears:-
    for Reynaud and Weygand:

Para 1:   Your comments will be examined
by General Staff who have orders to send the two
divisions as soon as possible. ,

            Permit me to observe that your divisions
picked out of Dunkirk are not to enter the line for
a month.   We are trying to send one of our
seasoned divisions in in a fortnight.

Para 2:   Fighter aircraft.   General Vuillemin's
demand was altogether unreasonable and his letter
made the worst impression on everyone here and
greatly increased my difficulties.   Kindly look at the
paragraph in which he refers to the assistance we
gave in the recent battle stop.   You don't seem
to understand at all the the British fighter aviation
has been worn to a shred and frightfully mixed up by
the need of material and prolonged standing patrols
over Dunkirk without which the evacuation would have
been impossible.   The mere sorting out of the

aeroplanes from the different squadrons practically
paralyses the force for four or five days.
However, I have sent you this morning a telegram
saying that we hold four squadrons of bombers
and two of Hurricane fighters available for
operations this afternoon and I shall try to
maintain the same tomorrow stop   You have no
right to ask us to deprive ourselves of the
sole means of continuing the war by casting
away in a single battle the already small forces
upon which we rely as the sole sure hope of
ultimate victory to us both.

5.6.40.

Prime Minister Winston Churchill, typewritten and signed letter with annotations, June 5, 1940.

Churchill to the President of France— The Desperate Final Days of the Battle of France
June 14, 1940
France Capitulated to Germany Two Days Later

"Your own declaration . . . about fighting before Paris, behind Paris, in a Province . . . in Africa or across the Atlantic. . . . [I exhort] France to continue the struggle [. . . and] not to miss this sovereign opportunity of bringing about the worldwide oceanic and economic coalition which must be fatal to Nazi domination. . . . We see . . . the light . . . at the end of the tunnel."

The morning of the day of this letter, in the War Cabinet meeting, Churchill approved the dispatch from Britain of fresh troops in an effort to keep alive French resistance. At the same time, he was realistically withdrawing British troops from danger in the center of France and planning a defensive perimeter in Brittany.

That morning Paris was lost; German troops had entered Paris, which had been declared an open city to protect it from bombardment and street fighting. Churchill turned his focus to keeping British troops in France, urging U.S. President Franklin Delano Roosevelt to send supplies, and plans for guerilla warfare.

-10, Downing Street, Whitehall.

Most Immediate.

Prime Minister to Monsieur Reynaud.

On returning here we received copy of President Roosevelt's answer to your appeal (stop) of June 10/ Cabinet is united in considering this magnificent document as decisive in favour of the continued resistance of France in accordance with your own declaration of June 10 about fighting before Paris, behind Paris, in a Province or if necessary in Africa or across the Atlantic (stop) The promise of redoubled material aid is coupled with definite advice and exhortation to France to continue the struggle even under the grievous conditions which you mentioned (stop) If France on this message of President Roosevelt's continues in the field and in the war we feel that the United States is committed beyond recall to take the only remaining step namely becoming a beligerent in form

Prime Minister Winston Churchill, typewritten letter, June 14, 1940.

Churchill was not giving up, as hour by hour, he exhorted French President Paul Reynaud and France to fight on everywhere, as he says in this message, "before Paris, behind Paris"—everywhere. By the end of the day he feared an armistice might be announced the next day, but did not let up in telling the French to never surrender, pleading with Roosevelt to announce aid and solidarity, negotiating with Parliament to announce a union with France, and telling Reynaud at 1:10 a.m. to "reply by first light."

It was a magnificent performance and effort of unequaled ferocity and commitment. It was everything he had embodied in his speech in Parliament 10 days earlier: "We shall fight in France, we shall fight on the beaches, we shall fight on the landing areas, we shall fight on the fields and streets, we shall fight in the hills, we shall never surrender."

Even Churchill's might could not stop the might of the Blitzkrieg. France surrendered two days later.

The Prime Minister writes a message to the Germans on a bomb shell.

G.R.

as she already has pre- constituted herself in fact (stop) Constitution of United States makes it impossible as you foresaw for President to declare war himself, but if you act on his advice and if he is not disavowed by the American people but if you act on his reply now received we sincerely believe that this must inevitably follow (stop) We are asking President to allow publication
even
of message but/if you act upon it- he does not agree to this for a day or two it is on the record and can afford the basis for your action (stop) I do beg you and your colleagues whose resolution we so much admired today not to miss this sovereign opportunity of bringing about the world-wide oceanic naval and economic coalition which must prevail to Nazi domination (stop) We see before us a definite plan of campaign and the light which you spoke of shines at the end of the tunnel.

14 13. VI

XI

Roosevelt's Message to the French President on the Fall of France
June 18, 1940

The causes of the Fall of France began years before Hitler unleashed his Blitzkrieg against Western Europe on May 10, 1940. France and England had spent the years since the end of the Great War, World War I, preparing to face another war with Germany—but it was the German Army from World War I that they were prepared for, and their military forces were led by generals from the First World War. Hitler, on the other hand, had modernized his military with much younger officers, new equipment, and tactics—specifically, lightening maneuvers and coordinating planes, tanks, and infantry.

France had built the impregnable Maginot Line protecting its border with Germany, somehow believing that Germany would not repeat what it had done in 1914—attack through the Ardennes into neutral Belgium. Hitler's May 10 attack focused on Holland and Belgium and he drew the British Army in France, and the French, into moving North to counterattack. The attack through the Ardennes— very difficult terrain consisting of many steep river valleys—cut off the British and French armies just south of Dunkirk. Those not evacuated by British boats were killed or taken prisoner. France and Paris were cut off. The Battle of France was over.

Washington, June 18, 1940

Your very deeply moving message has reached me and I wish to tell you how truly grateful I am for what you were good enough to say.

The American people will not forget the brilliant, courageous and effective resistance which you carried on at the head of your Government in the name of France.

The American people and their Government share the conviction that the ideals which France has exemplified for so many generations -- the ideals of human liberty, of democracy and of the highest form of human civilization -- will still triumph and that France herself will ultimately regain her full independence and freedom.

Franklin D. Roosevelt

President Franklin Delano Roosevelt, typewritten and signed letter, June 18, 1940.

Adolf Hitler poses in front of the Eiffel Tower with architect Albert Speer (left; see also no. 22) and artist Arno Breker, a week after France capitulates.

XII

Marshal Philippe Pétain's Annotated Draft of the French Armistice With Germany

"The Government of France orders the cessation of hostilities against the German Reich."

In mid-June 1940, France had no choice but surrender. The German Blitzkrieg had destroyed both the French and British armies and there was no realistic way that France could continue to resist. Paul Reynaud, the French Premier and ally of Churchill, in all respects, wanted to fight on to the end. His own cabinet was deeply divided; the World War I hero of Verdun, Marshal Pétain, was the leading proponent of an armistice and Reynaud had brought him back from his post as ambassador to Spain, making him Vice Premier. The 84-year-old Pétain accepted the Vice Premiership with the full knowledge that France could not win against Germany.

On June 11 Paris was declared an open city. On June 17 the French learned, many with relief, that their country would surrender to Germany within days. Hitler controlled his revenge, not occupying all of France and agreeing to neutralize the French Navy.

Hitler's sense of revenge was clear with the surrender ceremonies. He ordered the railroad car in which Germany had been forced to sign the armistice ending World War I to be brought from a French museum to Compiègne, where Germany had capitulated. Here, in the same car, Pétain signed the Armistice. Three days later, Hitler had the French monument marking this spot blown up and the railroad car taken to Berlin. It was destroyed in an air raid.

Marshal Philippe Pétain, typewritten draft of French Armistice (annotated), no date.

Marshal Henri Philippe Pétain.

Adolf Hitler (far left) listens to the preamble of the armistice with representatives from France on the same train car where the Germans surrendered in 1918.

XIII

The First Message
December 7, 1941

"AIRRAID ON PEARL HARBOR X THIS IS NO DRILL"

After she invaded and occupied China, the United States established an oil embargo of Japan. The United States refused to back down without Japanese withdrawal and Japan looked to the only source of oil within range—the Dutch East Indies. Fully aware that the U.S. and British navies would intercept any Japanese shipping if they attacked the Dutch East Indies, Japan determined to put both navies out of the war they were about to start. The plan was to attack everywhere in the Pacific at the same time. Singapore and Pearl Harbor were prime targets for the overall Japanese plan to succeed.

Japan faced daunting problems in attacking Pearl Harbor. The first was how to get their fleet close enough to Hawaii to launch carrier planes without being detected. Another was how to destroy the American Pacific Fleet in the shallow waters of Pearl Harbor. Conventional torpedoes needed much deeper water to operate and aerial bombs alone could not sink the battleships.

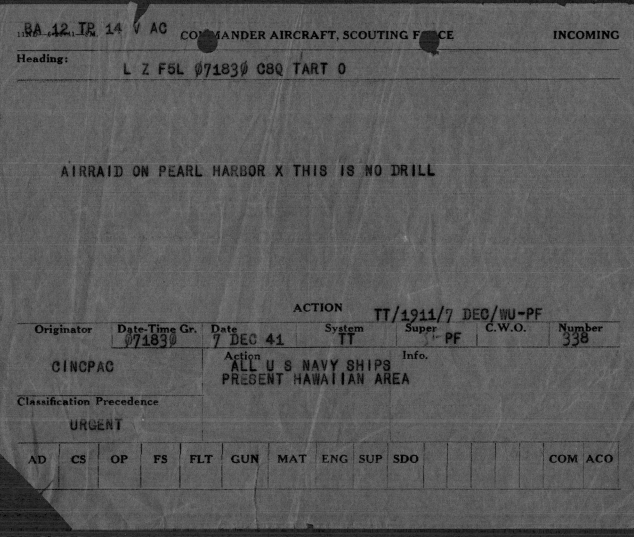

Telegram, December 7, 1941.

Technical breakthroughs by the Japanese developed shallow water torpedoes, and America's lack of respect for Japanese stealth and cunning provided the surprise.

The U.S. government knew that Japan was about to start the war and expected an attack almost anywhere in the Pacific. They never expected an attack on Hawaii. American opinion underestimated the Japanese; it did not occur to the government that Japan would be able to bring a naval fleet so close to Hawaii undetected. It was a bold move they did not think Japan was capable of accomplishing.

Because such an attack was unthinkable, the U.S. Navy missed every clear indication that the attack was underway. A Japanese mini-sub was spotted off the entrance to Pearl Harbor and the report was ignored; another was sunk, again without alarming the navy. The attacking Japanese airplanes were picked up on radar but this report was at first dismissed as a malfunction, and continued radar reports were dismissed as probably a flight of B-17s arriving ahead of schedule from California.

The Japanese seemed to do everything right and the U.S. Navy everything wrong on that historic and fateful morning. The Japanese planes quite amazingly did one thing very wrong: they failed to bomb the oil storage tanks and the dry docks. The fact that these survived gave the U.S. Navy the chance to turn the defeat around with one of the most—if not the most—remarkable recoveries in naval history. Six months later the U.S. Navy changed the course of the Pacific War with the defeat of the Imperial Japanese Navy at the Battle of Midway.

"Remember Pearl Harbor" became America's battle cry on the home front and the war fronts America never forgot it—just as importantly, the Japanese never did either.

Front page of the *Honolulu Star-Bulletin*, December 7, 1941.

Above: USS *Shaw* goes up in flames during the Japanese attack. Right: USS *West Virginia* (sunk), USS *Tennessee* (damaged), and USS *Arizona* (sunk).

XIV

Japan's Declaration of War Against the United States

By the grace of Heaven, Emperor of Japan. . . . We hereby declare War on the United States of America and the British Empire. The men and officers of Our Army and Navy shall do their utmost in prosecuting the war. Our public servants of various departments shall perform faithfully and diligently their respective duties; the entire nation with a united will shall mobilize their total strength so that nothing will miscarry in the attainment of Our war aims. To ensure the stability of East Asia and to contribute to world peace is the far-sighted policy.

On the afternoon of the surprise attack on Pearl Harbor, this declaration of war was read on Japanese radio. It was reprinted on the front page of every Japanese newspaper on the yearly anniversary of the attack, which brought America into World War II and ended the Empire of Japan.

Emperor Hirohito inspects the Japanese troops.

Japan's official declaration of war against the United States.

XV

The Secret Special Order for Douglas MacArthur and His Senior Staff to Be Evacuated by PT Boat From Corregidor as American Troops Are Forced to Surrender to the Japanese

Douglas MacArthur was Commander of American forces in the Philippines when the Japanese attacked Pearl Harbor. MacArthur was told that an attack on the Philippines was imminent but, in one of the war's most bizarre episodes, he sat frozen for hours, refusing to send out reconnaissance planes (which would have discovered Japanese carriers) or get planes into the air for defense. As a result, the entire air force in the Pacific was lost in the initial hours of the attack, and the Japanese landed the day after Pearl Harbor. Without air cover, the Americans, and the Philippine Army, were doomed.

They retreated to Corregidor, and by late February, MacArthur apparently believed he would die fighting with his men. On the last submarine to leave the fortress island he sent his trunk of personal possessions that he wanted to survive. General George C. Marshall had sent the submarine for MacArthur's wife and son, but Jean MacArthur had refused to leave her husband. MacArthur prepared to not be taken alive. Marshall decided, for military reasons, and Roosevelt for political reasons, that MacArthur had to be rescued. He was ordered to evacuate, but the Japanese were closing in too rapidly for another submarine to reach Corregidor. Three PT boats were still serviceable; and they prepared to take MacArthur to the southern Philippines, and then he would be flown to Australia.

Official U.S. Army document, stamped "SECRET," dated March 11, 1942.

Not to be superseded by his commander, General Marshall, MacArthur changed the evacuation order, which specified that only MacArthur would be evacuated, to include his wife and son,13 army officers, two naval officers, and a staff sergeant. In a very controversial decision he included his family's nanny.

MacArthur's fate was being discussed in Washington and it was clear the Japanese were preparing to stop him. His departure was moved up to March 11, the date of this document, which has notations in pencil as to which PT boat each person was to go in. Notably, MacArthur's family and nanny are not listed.

On May 6 the surviving Americans were forced to surrender. The Bataan Death March and years of starvation and beatings followed for those that survived.

American and Philippine troops surrender to the Japanese.

MacArthur awards the Distinguished Service Cross to the Philippine Air Force's Captain Jesús A. Villamor, for his heroic service in the Battle of Bataan.

XVI

Erwin Rommel Shows His Genius for Battlefield Tactics in a Lengthy, Illustrated, and Heavily Detailed Combat Report

In World War I, Erwin Rommel showed both bravery and tactical genius. He was wounded three times, was awarded both First and Second Class Iron Crosses, and, as seen in this manuscript, had great ability and interest in combat tactics. In 1937 he wrote a military classic, *Infantry Attacks,* about his World War I experiences. It was read by commanders on both sides.

In this manuscript report, dated June, 1918, Rommel describes in great detail, and with many maps, the battle that took place on October 24, 1917, in which the Italians were routed, retreating all the way back to the Piave. In one part of the report, after fighting all day, Rommel's forces climb a steep incline in the dark and follow the yelling of the retreating Italian troops. "The enemy troops . . . have to surrender in spite of themselves. First a few come, then the whole regiment with all the officers. The colonel almost collapses and weeps in embarrassment."

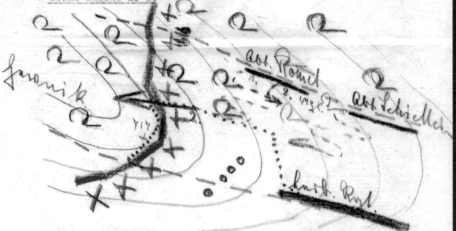

Senior Lieutenant Erwin Rommel, typewritten document (annotated), June 1918.

A young Erwin Rommel.

XVII

El Alamein—
The Original Manuscript of One of the Most Famous Messages by Any Military Commander Before One of the Most Decisive Battles in History
October 23, 1942

Bernard Montgomery commanded the British forces in North Africa, which drove Rommel's forces from Egypt, Libya, and Tripolitania. This autographed manuscript is signed: Middle East Forces, October 23, 1942. It is headed: "EIGHTH ARMY / Personal Message from the Army Commander."

Montgomery wrote this message just hours before the opening of the Battle of El Alamein, to be read to the more than 150,000 troops under his command.

1. When I assumed command of the Eighth Army I said that the mandate was to destroy ROMMELL and his army, and that it would be done as soon as we were ready.

2. We are ready now. The battle which is now about to begin will be one of the decisive battles of history; it will be the turning point of the war. The eyes of the whole world will be on us, watching anxiously which way the battle will swing. We can give them their answer at once: "It will swing our way."

3. We have first class equipment; good tanks; good anti-tank guns; plenty of artillery and plenty of ammunition; and we are backed up by the finest Air Striking Force in the world. All that is necessary is that each one of us, every officer and man, should enter this battle with the determination to see it through—to fight and to kill—and finally to win. If we all do this there can be only one result—together we will hit the enemy . . . right out of North Africa.

Lieutenant General Bernard Montgomery, handwritten and signed letter, October 23, 1942.

4. The sooner we win this battle, which will be the turning point of this war, the sooner we shall all get back home to our families.

5. Therefore let every officer and man enter the battle with a stout heart, and with the determination to do his duty so long as he has breath in his body. AND LET NO MAN SURRENDER SO LONG AS HE IS UNWOUNDED AND CAN FIGHT.

The successful advance of General Erwin Rommel's Afrika Korps across North Africa in 1942 came to a halt in Egypt at El Alamein, about 60 miles west of Alexandria. His combined German and Italian forces, by that point, numbered some 96,000 men, with less than 600 tanks, artillery, and planes still operational. Montgomery's forces by then numbered some 150,000 men—British, Australian, New Zealander, and South African—along a 40-mile front, armed with over 1,000 tanks, nearly 2,200 artillery pieces, and the use of 500 fighter aircraft and 200 bombers.

The battle opened at 9:40 p.m. on October 23 with a 1,000-gun barrage along a six-mile front near the coast—a barrage of unprecedented intensity. Twenty minutes later, under a full moon, two corps attacked the Axis forces to the right and, in a diversionary maneuver, to the south. The pattern of Allied advances—with Montgomery's novel method of allowing infantry to clear a path for tanks—and Axis counterattacks (neutralized to a large extent by Royal Air Force bombing) continued for 13 days, until—despite Hitler's frantic command that Rommel should hold at all cost—the entire German and Italian front crumbled and their forces turned in full retreat. Montgomery's losses (which he had predicted with remarkable accuracy) were 13,000 killed, wounded, and captured, with 430 tanks disabled. Rommel's losses were about 50,000 men and a massive quantity of artillery and tanks.

Although Montgomery's pursuit of Rommel's forces and the combined Allied offensives continued for many hard months,

Lieutenant General Montgomery watches his tanks move up during the Battle of El Alamein.

with many more fierce battles, before the Axis hold on North Africa was finally broken (in May 1943, when 275,000 troops surrendered in Tunisia), the Battle of El Alamein was indeed, precisely as Montgomery said in his inspiring message to the Eighth Army, the turning point of the war. In terms of its scale and consequences, both strategic and psychological, it was scarcely an exaggeration for him to predict that it would be one of the most decisive battles in history.

Within a week of the Battle of El Alamein, in a speech on November 10, 1942, Churchill declared, "This is not the end. It is not even the beginning of the end. But it is perhaps the end of the beginning," and he could say later that before Alamein there were no victories; after Alamein there was nothing but victories. Seemingly invincible German armies had at last suffered a defeat. The morale of the Allied public soared as never before; Axis morale suffered a corresponding decline; and Montgomery, the first victorious British general of the war, became a national hero overnight.

XVIII

Bernard Montgomery's Message to the 8th Army on the Capture of Tripoli and the Defeat of Erwin Rommel
January 23, 1943

"The defeat of the enemy in battle at Alamein, the pursuit of his beaten army, and the final capture of Tripoli . . . is probably without parallel in history."

This is Bernard Montgomery's original autographed manuscript from which the message was printed for distribution to officers and read to the British 8th Army troops.

1. Today, 23 January [1943], exactly three months after we began the battle of Egypt, the Eighth Army has captured TRIPOLI and has driven the enemy away to the west towards TUNISIA. By skillful withdrawal tactics the enemy has eluded us, though we have taken heavy toll of his army and air forces.
2. The defeat of the enemy in battle at ALAMEIN, the pursuit of his beaten army, and the final capture of TRIPOLI—a distance of some 1,400 miles from ALAMEIN—has all been accomplished in three months. This achievement is probably without parallel in history; it could not have been done unless every soldier in the Army had pulled his full weight all the time. I congratulate the whole Army, and send my personal thanks to each one of you for the wonderful support you have given me.

General Bernard Montgomery, handwritten and signed letter, January 23, 1943.

3. On your behalf I have sent a special message to the Allied Air Forces that have cooperated with us. I don't suppose that any Army has ever been supported by such a magnificent air striking force. I have always maintained that the Eighth Army and the R.A.F. Western Desert together constitute one fighting machine, and therein lies our great strength.

Once again I thank you all from the bottom of my heart.

Tripoli, the last of the Italian overseas possessions, was the first major enemy town captured by the Allies since the beginning of the Second World War, and its surrender on the day this message was issued resulted in the immediate removal of Rommel from the post of Commander of the German-Italian Panzer Army. In a letter to Field Marshal Harold Alexander, dated November 18, 1942, Montgomery had stated the most urgent objectives after the victory of El Alamein: "If the enemy wants to remain in N. Africa he requires the use of Tripoli. Our object is to remove the Axis forces from N. Africa; therefore an essential step in this direction must be the capture, or complete neutralization, of Tripoli."

General Montgomery, Tripoli, January 27, 1943.

3

4. In the hour of success we must not forget the splendid work that has been done by those soldiers working day and night in back areas and on the lines of communication. There are many soldiers quietly doing their duty in rear areas who are unable to take part in the triumphal entry into captured cities; but they are a vital part of our fighting machine and we could gain no successes if they failed to pull their full weight. I refer especially to stevedores at our bases, to fitters in the workshops, to clerks in rear offices, and so on. I would like to make a special mention of our R.A.S.C. drivers; these men drive long distances by day and night for long periods; they are always cheerful; and they always deliver the goods. The R.A.S.C. has risen to great

4

heights during the operations we have undertaken, and as a Corps it deserves the grateful thanks of every soldier in the Army.

5. There is much work still in front of us. But I know that you are all ready for any task that we may be called on to carry out.

6. Once again I thank you all from the bottom of my heart.

23 Jan 1943

B. L. MONTGOMERY
General
G.O.C. - in - C
Eighth Army.

XIX

George S. Patton Writes to His Father as a New West Point Cadet

"I hope . . . war is still feasible and there will be more wars."

men made a great fuss about being under a nigger, truly they are logical in their opinions of Southerners.

I saw some plebes walking through the area with some girls the third class men were very polite but tonight O lord.

I am very much disheartened by the wonderful efficiency of the modern rifle and there is now talk of making a gun which fires 20 shots a second. I dont exactly see how war is to be carried on against such abstacles abstacles but

UNITED STATES MILITARY ACADEMY
WEST POINT, NEW YORK

and when Cap Thompson saw the Juck, in charge of us saw it he took me out of ranks and sent me to the hospital because he thought that the bites were poison oak or chicken-pox. They kept me at the hospital two days and let me sleep all I wished; it was a snap I think I will get a pet bedbug - One of the cadet officers who has been over us is an Hawaian and he looks like a nigger the northern

George S. Patton, handwritten and signed letter, no date.

I am very much disheartened by the wonderful efficiency of the modern rifle and there is now talk of them making a gun which fires 20 shots a second. I don't exactly see how war is to be carried on against such obstacles but . . . I will try. . . . the story of a rapid fire gun may be entirely a mith [sic]. I hope it is, for if it is, war is still feasible and there will be more wars.

George S. Patton's grandfather had been a Civil War general and his father had worked tirelessly to get him an appointment to West Point. Patton, suffering from dyslexia, had entered the Virginia Military Institute in September 1903 to prepare for West Point, and in March 1904 he was nominated after scoring the highest marks in the competitive exam in his home state of California. He had enrolled at West Point just 10 days before he wrote, at 18 years old, this letter to the father who had greatly influenced him.

George S. Patton, pictured as a cadet at West Point.

XX

George S. Patton to the Sultan of Morocco Two Days After the Landings in Casablanca
November 10, 1942

Your Majesty must realize the painful sentiments which I entertain in contemplating the necessity of shedding the blood of my friends, but the stern necessity of war demands that if the French armed forces continue to demonstrate the hostility they have already shown, it is my military duty and purpose to attack by air, by sea, and by land, with the utmost violence known to modern war.

North Africa was the first entry of Americans into combat during World War II. Patton commanded the American forces landing in Casablanca on November 8, 1942. Patton's diplomatic skills were called on in the negotiations with the French forces there who were, through the Vichy French government, allied with Germany. The day Patton wrote this letter to the Sultan of Morocco, the Commander-in-Chief of the Vichy French Armed Forces, Admiral François Darlan, agreed to a cease-fire. This saved Casablanca from the destruction that Patton told the Sultan would result if there was no agreement. Germany reacted by occupying Vichy France, and ending any semblance of an independent France.

HEADQUARTERS WESTERN TASK FORCE
CITY OF FEDALA

November 10, 1942

His Majesty the Sultan of Morocco

Your Majesty:

Owing to the stress of battle, this is the first time I have had the opportunity of explaining to Your Majesty the purpose of the American operations in Morocco.

In keeping with the ancient and traditional friendship of the Government and People of the United States of America for the Person of Your Majesty and his People, as well as for the Government of France, my forces have landed in your country in irresistable numbers. We desired to come among you as friends, not as conquerors, not as enemies. Our purpose is to protect your Throne and your Country, and the people of France in Morocco, against their enslavement by our common enemy—the Nazis, and to maintain your authority and the French civil authority, and to insure to You and your People the continued orderly government which you formerly enjoyed.

As Your Majesty knows, the President of the United States has stated on his "Word of Honor" to all the world that as soon as our common enemy is destroyed, we shall leave your country, nor shall we demand of You or your People anything other than friendship. In His name I hereby guarantee that if you offer no resistance, your religious institutions, your customs, and your laws will be completely respected, and that at the termination of hostilities with the Nazis, Morocco will be returned to you and to the civil government of France in exactly the same state that it was before this war.

Your Majesty must realize the painful sentiments which I entertain in contemplating the necessity of shedding the blood of my friends, but the stern necessity of war demands that if the French armed forces continue to demonstrate the hostility they have already shown, it is my military duty and purpose to attack by air, by sea, and by land, with the utmost violence known to modern war.

It must be evident to you that in the course of such an attack the beautiful cities of your beloved country must inevitably suffer irreparable injury because when once serious battle is joined I cannot be responsible for the consequences.

It is my respectful opinion that it is your duty as a patriot, as a ruler, and as a long time friend of America to use all your power to see that this fratricidal strife terminates at once. It is imperative in order to avoid the unnecessary shedding of blood that a statement of amity by you and by the French armed forces be provided to me by 12:00 midnight tonight Morocco time. Time is vital as my preparations are complete.

I have the honor, Your Majesty, to remain,

G. S. PATTON, JR.,
Major General, U. S. Army,
Commanding American Forces in Morocco

Major General George S. Patton, typewritten letter, November 10, 1942

Major General George Patton with King Mohammed V of Morocco, November 1942.

XXI

Joseph Stalin's Detailed Analysis of Russia's Positions
November 13, 1942

I am answering the questions you sent me on November 12: 1. "How does the Soviet side assess the Allied campaign in Africa?" Answer. The Soviet side regards this campaign as a significant fact of great import which demonstrates the growing power of the Allied forces and opens a perspective of the disintegration of the Italo-German coalition in a short time. The campaign in Africa once again refutes the skeptics who claim that the English-American leadership is incapable of organizing a serious military operation. There may be no doubt that only first-class organizers could carry out such major military operations as the successful ocean landings in North Africa, the rapid conquest of ports and further territory from Casablanca to *Bejaïa*, and the brilliantly executed destruction of the Italo-German forces in the western desert. 2. "How effective is this campaign in regard to reducing pressure on the Soviet Union and what further assistance does the Soviet Union expect?" Answer. It is still too early to speak of the effectiveness of this campaign in regard to the reduction of military pressure on the Soviet Union. But it can be said with conviction that the effect will not be small and that this lessening of pressure on the Soviet Union will set in very shortly. But that is not the only thing. Primarily it means that inasmuch as the campaign in Africa signifies a transition of the initiative into the hands of our allies, it changes the military and political situation in Europe fundamentally to the advantage of the English-Soviet-American coalition. It undermines the authority of

- 2 -

руки наших союзников, она меняет в корне военно-политическое положение в Европе в пользу англо-советско-американской коалиции. Она подрывает авторитет гитлеровской Германии, как руководящей силы в системе государств оси и деморализует союзников Гитлера в Европе. Она выводит Францию из состояния оцепенения, мобилизует антигитлеровские силы Франции и дает базу для организации антигитлеровской французской армии. Она создает условия для вывода из строя Италии и для изоляции гитлеровской Германии. Наконец, она создает предпосылки для организации второго фронта в Европе поближе к жизненным центрам Германии, что будет иметь решающее значение в деле организации победы над гитлеровской тиранией.

3. "Какова вероятность присоединения советской наступательной силы на Востоке к союзникам на Западе в целях ускорения окончательной победы?"

Ответ. Можно не сомневаться в том, что Красная Армия выполнит с честью свою задачу, так же как она выполняла ее на протяжении всей войны.

Москва, 13 ноября 1942 г.

Premier Joseph Stalin, typewritten and signed letter, November 13, 1942.

Hitler's Germany as the leading power in the system of states of the Axis Powers and demoralizes Hitler's European allies. It brings France out of her state of paralysis, mobilizes France's anti-Hitler factions, and forms a basis for the organization of a French army against Hitler. It creates the preconditions for luring Italy out of its alliance and isolating Hitler's Germany. Finally, it creates the preconditions for organizing a second European front nearer the vital centers of Germany, which will take on crucial importance in organizing the victory over Hitler's tyranny. 3. "How great is the probability of a uniting of Soviet offensive forces in the East with the Allies in the West to speed up the final victory?" Answer. There can be no doubt that the Red Army is fulfilling its task with honor, just as it has done during the entire war. [Joseph Stalin. Typewritten Letter Signed, *With utmost esteem, J. Stalin*, Moscow, November 13, 1942. In Cyrillic, to the Associated Press reporter in Moscow, Henry Cassidy.]

When Stalin wrote his responses to Henry Cassidy's questions, Montgomery's attack at El Alamein, which had begun on October 23, had caused Rommel's forces to begin their retreat to the Mareth Line within the frontiers of Tunisia. At the same time, the Axis position in Tunisia was being battered from the west, through the execution of "Torch." Meanwhile, on Russian soil, the German offensive on Stalingrad was taking place. The most critical moment had taken place on October 14, when Soviet defenders had their backs so close to the Volga that the few remaining supply crossings of the river came under German machine-gun fire. The huge Soviet counteroffensive launched on November 19–20 proved to be the turning point of the military struggle between Germany and the Soviet Union. The battle used up precious German reserves, destroyed two entire armies, and humiliated the prestigious German war machine.

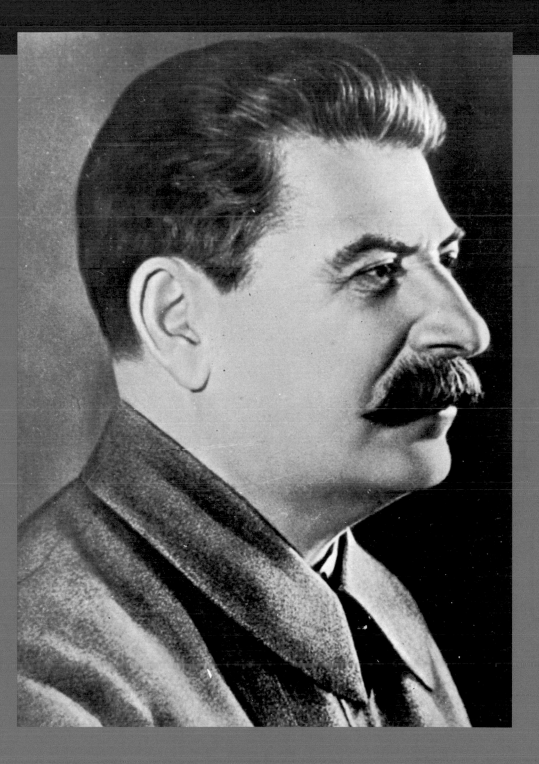

XXII

Hitler's Most Important Appointment of the War—
Albert Speer Replaces Fritz Todt, Hitler's Building and Construction Czar, the Day After Todt's Plane Explodes
February 8, 1942

Albert Speer had accepted Fritz Todt's offer of a seat on his flight to Berlin from Hitler's "Wolf's Lair" (headquarters at Rastenburg, in East Prussia). Hitler, at 1:00 that morning, had summoned Speer and they had talked most of the night, causing Speer to cancel going to Berlin. Todt's plane mysteriously blew up on takeoff and, later on the 8th, Hitler told Speer that he would replace Todt in his three major positions, including Inspector General of Water and Energy. The next day, the three appointments were prepared, including this one, and Hitler presented them to Speer.

The appointment of Speer to succeed Todt is considered one of Hitler's shrewdest decisions.

Albert Speer had been an intimate of Hitler as his architect, designing and building the new government buildings intended to display the power and might of the new Germany. Speer also designed and choreographed the Nürnberg rallies with their tremendous propaganda impact. Speer created the "Cathedral of Ice" at Nürnberg with the hundreds of air-raid search lights ringing the stadium pointed straight up into the night sky.

With this appointment, and the two others the same day, Speer took over all industrial production in Germany, carefully and brilliantly maneuvering through the

Im Namen
des
Deutschen Volkes

ernenne ich

den Generalbauinspektor für die Reichshauptstadt

Diplom-Ingenieur Professor

A l b e r t   S p e e r

zum Generalinspektor für Wasser und Energie.

Führer-Hauptquartier, den 9. Februar 1942.

Der Führer

labyrinth of political factions to increase armaments production despite the Allied air raids on Germany. Speer is credited with prolonging the war with his genius for organization, administration, and political infighting. He changed his course in early 1945 when he realized the war was lost and subverted Hitler's orders to destroy Germany's remaining industrial base. He narrowly escaped SS assassination. At the Nürnberg war trials he was the only one of the 20 defendants to show an understanding and regret for his role in the Third Reich. As a result, he was spared the death penalty given to most of the defendants, and served 20 years.

Adolf Hitler and Albert Speer.

XXIII

The Most Revealing Letter of a Commander-in-Chief in Wartime— Dwight Eisenhower to His Wife
February 15, 1943

My dearest,

...Your telegram of congratulations on my latest (and final possible) promotion came just before I left my headquarters. Strangely enough, my first news of the incident came from the British Broadcasting Co. I wouldn't believe it, although I knew the matter was under consideration at home. I knew also that General G.C.M. [Marshall] wanted to do it—but I was in no position to know whether or not the newspaper argument that developed out of some of the moves here might have made my promotion politically inexpedient. Actually, I didn't have much feeling about it. . . . I am human enough to want the official approval of my past action that such an unusual advancement implies—but anyone worthy of high command is so concerned with the enormity of the tasks, for which his own faculties so frequently seem pitifully inadequate, that what the world calls success or promotion does not loom up as particularly important. I do not often write to you of my responsibilities, it comes down to something like this. Most jobs in the world are such that the responsible man always has at his shoulders, a higher authority to whom a particularly serious decision can be referred. A few jobs are such that this can scarcely ever be done. My technical boss is a combined body of men (8) that is divided into two parts by the Atlantic Ocean. Moreover, an active theater of war must be commanded on the spot. So the boss in that one has only one real confidant—his pillow, and only the underneath side of that! Loneliness is the inescapable lot of a man holding such a job. Subordinates can advise, urge, help and

General Dwight D. Eisenhower, handwritten and signed letter, February 15, 1943.

pray—but only one man, in his own mind and heart, can decide "Do we, or do we not?" The stakes are always highest, and the penalties are expressed in terms of loss of life or major or minor disasters to the nation. No man can always be right. So the struggle is to do one's best; to keep the brain and conscience clear; never to be swayed by unworthy motives or inconsequential reasons, but to strive to unearth the basic factors involved and then do one's duty. It is not always easy—in fact the strain comes from not being sure that the analysis has been carefully and accurately made. And when it is clear that the only logical answer is certain to bring criticism; even possible official misunderstanding by superiors; then is when such things as popularity, favorable press, possible promotion, etc. etc., must be completely disregarded—I'm simply trying to say that in a job like this so many things are so big that even a fourth star fails to cause any great internal excitement. I appreciate the confidence of my superiors—and feel damn humble in the face of it, but I do not feel that my major job is finished. I've just begun and though the prospect is, in some phases, appalling, I can do my duty only if I steel myself to the requirements and meet them to the best of my ability. When you remember me in your prayers, that's the special thing I want—always to do my duty to the extreme limit of my ability.

The day before this letter Rommel's forces had hit the American lines, where Ike had been only hours before, and the lines had crumbled. Eisenhower returned to Constantine to plan the new defense to block Rommel's offense, which became known as "Kasserine Pass." It was the Americans' first combat, and they were soundly beaten by the "Desert Fox."

2

It is not always easy — in fact the strain comes from not being sure that the analysis has been carefully and accurately made. And when it is clear that the only logical answer is certain to bring criticism; even possibly official misunderstanding by superiors; then is when such things as popularity, favorable press, possible promotion, etc etc must be so completely disregarded as the ant crawling across the floor. I hope that even my most violent critics (of which I understand there are some, though I rarely see any news item from home) thinks I am or was so stupid as to fail to realize that acceptance of Darlan would be bitterly assailed by many, particularly by those who think that all humans think in terms of self only. The same ones are now probably giving me the devil for not having captured Tunisia — but I wonder where those people think my front lines would now be if I had not accepted the poor Darlan at that moment? I'm not — and never have — attempted to defend anything; not even to you — I'm simply trying to say that in a job like this so many things are so big that even a fourth star fail to cause any great internal excitement. I appreciate the confidence of my superiors — and I feel damned humble in the face of it, but I do not feel that I've "arrived" — or that my major job is finished. I've just begun and though the prospect is, in some phases, appalling, I can do my duty only if I steel myself to the requirements and meet them to the best of my ability. When you remember me in your prayers, that's the special thing I want — always to do

(over)

my duty to the extreme limit of my ability.

The present intense activity on the front will have been reported through the newspapers long before you get this. I feel I've good subordinates on the job — and I firmly believe we'll give a good account of ourselves. Finally we'll win — but we cannot afford bad mistake or any complacency. We must think clearly, strike rapidly and never give up! Eternal energy, intelligently applied is what I need — as do all other americans and our allies.

I hope this letter does not sound morbid. I don't mean it so + I love you so much that I always like you to realize exactly how I feel about things; and for some reason I felt like attempting to explain today. I try to keep fit, optimistic and calm —. Both my temper and my disposition are sometimes sorely tried, but I think I do a pretty good job of controlling both, even if poor Ernest & Mickey sometimes suffer a bit. They know I don't mean to hurt their feelings, so occasionally they have to let me blow off. Secretly, I think an outburst on my part amuses rather than alarms them.

Did I say "I love you"? Well I do — & how I hope you are taking care of your health & are as happy as possible. I want you to extract all the pleasure you can, consistent with doing the things you feel you should — but no matter what you do, please don't forget me. Always your —

Ike

XXIV

The Journal of the Fighter Pilot Who Shot Down Admiral Yamamoto's Plane, and His Map of the Mission
April 1943

Captain Tom Lanphier.

Fighter pilot Captain Tom Lanphier, in his journal beginning April 17, 1943, described the meeting on Guadalcanal at which he and others were briefed for their top-secret mission of intercepting Yamamoto's plane, which would be protected by six Zero fighters. Eighteen P-38's were to intercept Yamamoto's group the next morning. They would take a very roundabout route, "clear of any island where we could be seen by the Japs." Commander John W. Mitchell designated four fighter pilots, including Lanphier, to go after Yamamoto's plane. A complex plan was worked out, "and success would also depend on Admiral Yamamoto's arriving on time, as we had only 15 minutes over the target area. Intelligence has it that there are between 75 and 100 Zero's at Kahila Airfield so it will have to be fast in and out."

When American intelligence learned of Yamamoto's planned air trip in April 1943, it was a major decision to risk the Japanese realizing that their naval code was being read versus the benefit of killing Japan's most important naval strategist.

Yamamoto's party consisted of two Mitsubishi "Betty" bombers, in addition to the fighters, and Lanphier went after the first. "At 6100 feet I rolled over and dove at full power on a Betty I saw fleeing south just above the trees. I approached from 3 o'clock and fired a long burst of fire. . . . The fire quickly spread to the wing which sheared off as the Betty hit the jungle. While I was firing . . . Rex Barber went straight for the second Betty and fired, completely destroying the tail, causing it to crash into the jungle."

Admiral Yamamoto was opposed to war with the United States and as a senior naval officer made his views widely known. He knew America from having attended Harvard and serving in Washington. Once Japan decided to attack, Yamamoto was vociferous in his

Captain Tom Lanphier, handwritten journal, beginning April 17, 1943.

belief that Japan's only hope was to destroy the U.S. Pacific Fleet in Pearl Harbor and conquer all of Southeast Asia before America could rebuild. He knew Japan could not win a war against American production.

The surprise attack on Pearl Harbor, on December 7, was Yamamoto's bold plan against considerable naval opposition who thought it too risky. The attack on Midway, six months later, was also his brainchild, but America's breaking of the Japanese naval code caused a crushing defeat of the Japanese Navy.

The death of Yamamoto was the first public recognition in Japan of any wartime reversal. His funeral in Tokyo was a major event.

XXV

Franklin Roosevelt's Telegrams to Josef Stalin Arranging to Meet at the Tehran Conference and Afterward Reiterating His View of the Success of the Conference
November 12 and December 2, 1943

The Tehran Conference, November 28 to December 1, 1943, was the first meeting of Roosevelt, Churchill, and Stalin. Stalin stressed the importance of a second front with an invasion of France to relieve the Soviets fighting the Germans on their own soil. Roosevelt and Churchill agreed to invade France in May 1944, and Stalin agreed to mount a major offensive against the Germans at the same time. He also agreed to join the war against Japan as soon as Germany was defeated.

President Franklin D. Roosevelt, handwritten and signed message, November 12, 1943.

November 12, 1943: "I am of course made very happy by your telegram . . . and the definite prospect of our meeting. . . . I shall be very glad to see Mr. Molotov in Cairo on the 22nd. I am just leaving for French North Africa. . . ."

SECRET   December 2, 1943.

From: The President.
To :   Marshal Stalin.

    I have arrived safely at my destination and earnestly
hope that by this time you have done the same. I consider that
the conference was a great success and I am sure that it was an
historic event in the assurance not only of our ability to wage
war together but to work in the utmost harmony for the peace to
come. I enjoyed very much our personal talks together and
particularly the opportunity of meeting you face to face. I
look forward to seeing you again. In the meantime I wish your
armies the greatest success.

                        ROOSEVELT.

President Roosevelt, typewritten and signed message, December 2, 1943.

Stalin, Roosevelt, and Churchill at the Tehran Conference.

XXVI

George Patton's Battle Map of Sicily

The Allies' invasion of Sicily involved 180,000 troops; it was commanded by British General Harold Alexander. Bernard Montgomery was given the major role, with George Patton ordered to protect his flank, as Montgomery was expected to move quickly to block the Axis troops from withdrawing to the mainland from Messina.

Montgomery's very slow progress enabled Patton to constantly exceed his intended lines of advance, and instead of protecting Montgomery's advance, Patton's aggressive and lightning strikes took the entire island, including Palermo, before arriving in Messina ahead of Montgomery.

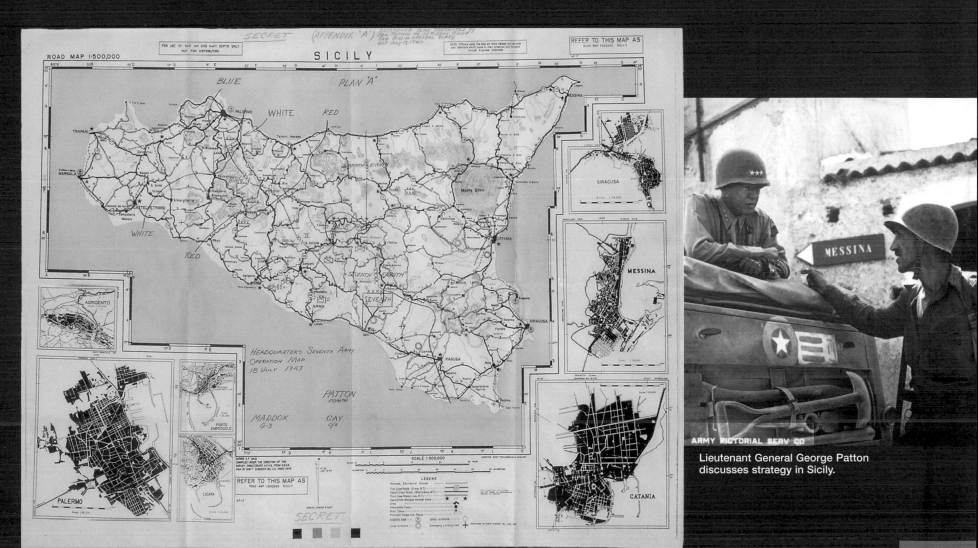

Lieutenant General George Patton discusses strategy in Sicily.

Patton Demands the Surrender of Palermo, Ending the Sicilian Campaign

"In the name of Lieut General G. S. Patton, Jr., Commanding the Seventh United States Army, I hereby call upon you to surrender unconditionally all Axis troops and individuals, ground, air or naval under your command regardless of nationality, with the city of Palermo, and territory adjacent thereto.

"Failure on your part to accept this demand immediately will result in the attack by ground, air and sea by my superior forces, and the destruction of Palermo, the useless loss of life, and the imposition of hardship and suffering upon many innocent persons."

Major General Geoffrey Keyes, handwritten letter signed on behalf of Lieutenant General George S. Patton, no date.

XXVII

The Armistice Agreement Between Italy and the United States,
Signed by Eisenhower's Chief of Staff and the Representative of Mussolini's Successor
September 3, 1943

As the Allied Armies began to envelop Sicily from both coasts, the Fascist government of Italy overthrew Mussolini on July 25, 1943, and appointed Marshal Pietro Badoglio as his successor. The Allies captured Messina, Sicily, on August 17 and began to prepare the assault on the Italian mainland.

Badoglio wanted to negotiate secretly with the Allies while keeping Germany at bay; the Italians wanted the armistice to coincide with a massive Anglo-American landing on the mainland backed by Italian troops. Meanwhile, the Germans, aware of Italian intentions, increased their troop strength in Italy from six divisions in July to 12 in September.

This armistice, seen here, was announced September 8, and the Allies landed at Salerno the next day, beginning the extremely arduous and costly campaign up the mainland of Italy.

The following conditions of an Armistice are presented by General DWIGHT D. EISENHOWER, Commander-in-Chief of the Allied Forces, acting by authority of the Goverments of the United States and Great Britain and in the interest of the United Nations, and are accepted by Marshal PIETRO BADOGLIO Head of the Italian Government.

Marshal Pietro Badoglio

FAIRFIELD CAMP,

SICILY.

September 3rd, 1943.

The following conditions of an Armistice are presented by

General DWIGHT D. EISENHOWER,

Commander-in-Chief of the Allied Forces,

acting by authority of the Governments of the United States and
Great Britain and in the interest of the United Nations, and
are accepted by

Marshal PIETRO BADOGLIO

Head of the Italian Government.

1. Immediate cessation of all hostile activity by the
Italian armed forces.

2. Italy will use its best endeavors to deny, to the Germans,
facilities that might be used against the United Nations.

3. All prisoners or internees of the United Nations to be
immediately turned over to the Allied Commander in Chief, and
none of these may now or at any time be evacuated to Germany.

4. Immediate transfer of the Italian Fleet and Italian
aircraft to such points as may be designated by the Allied
Commander in Chief, with details of disarmament to be prescribed
by him.

5. Italian merchant shipping may be requisitioned by the
Allied Commander in Chief to meet the needs of his military -
naval program.

6. Immediate surrender of Corsica and of all Italian
territory, both islands and mainland, to the Allies, for such use
as operational bases and other purposes as the Allies may see
fit.

7. Immediate guarantee of the free use by the Allies of all
airfields and naval ports in Italian territory, regardless of
the rate of evacuation of the Italian territory by the German
forces. These ports and fields to be protected by Italian armed
forces until this function is taken over by the Allies.

8. Immediate/.....

1. Immediate cessation of all hostile activity by the Italian armed forces.
2. Italy will use its best endeavors to deny, to the Germans, facilities that might be used against the United Nations.
3. All prisoners or internees of the United Nations to be immediately turned over to the Allied Commander in Chief, and none of these may now or at any time be evacuated to Germany.
4. Immediate transfer of the Italian Fleet and Italian aircraft to such points as may be designated by the Allied Commander in Chief, with details of disarmament to be prescribed by him.
5. Italian merchant shipping may be requisitioned by the Allied Commander in Chief to meet the needs of his military-naval program.
6. Immediate surrender of Corsica and of all Italian territory, both islands and mainland, to the Allies, for such use as operational bases and other purposes as the Allies may see fit.
7. Immediate guarantee of the free use by the Allies of all airfields and naval ports in Italian territory, regardless of the rate of evacuation of the Italian territory by the German forces. These ports and fields to be protected by Italian armed forces until this function is taken over by the Allies.

Official document, signed by Marshal Pietro Badoglio and General Dwight D. Eisenhower.

8. Immediate withdrawal to Italy of Italian armed forces from all participation in the current war from whatever areas in which they may be now engaged.

9. Guarantee by the Italian Government that if necessary it will employ all its available armed forces to insure prompt and exact compliance with all the provisions of this armistice.

10. The Commander in Chief of the Allied Forces reserves to himself the right to take any measure which in his opinion may be necessary for the protection of the interests of the Allied Forces for the prosecution of the war, and the Italian Government binds itself to take such administrative or other action as the Commander in Chief may require, and in particular the Commander in Chief may require, and in particular the Commander in Chief will establish Allied Military Government over such parts of Italian territory as he may deem necessary in the military interests of the Allied Nations.

11. The Commander in Chief of the Allied Forces will have a full right to impose measures of disarmament, demobilization and demilitarization.

12. Other conditions of a political, economic and financial nature with which Italy will be bound to comply will be transmitted at a later date.

The conditions of the present Armistice will not be made public without prior approval of the Allied Commander in Chief. The English will be considered the official text.

Signing the armistice between Italy and the Allies: Eisenhower's Chief of Staff, General Walter Bedell Smith, is seated; General Giuseppe Castellano, representing Mussolini's successor, Badoglio, is at the end of the table (in dark suit).

XXVIII

Dwight Eisenhower to His Wife
December 4, 1943

"I know I'm a changed person—no one could be through what I've seen and not be different from what he was at the beginning."

Darling—A few days ago I sent you a bracelet of silver, made in this country. You may never wear it, but it can be a souvenir of this region. Now I'm sending you a little bracelet (identification tags in gold) a couple pairs of silk socks and a pair of white leather gloves. The bracelet has my initials on it and was sent to me by a woman in the U.S. of whom I've never heard. I have no use for it, but thought you might value it as a trinket. Of course you'll have to accept it as a "secret" gift, my dear—because this woman might learn that I had not held on to her gift. I miss you terribly. What is going to happen as a result of all rumored changes in command, etc. I don't know. But no matter what does happen—I do hope I can have a visit with you before too long. I know I'm a changed person—no one could be through what I've seen and not be different from what he was at the beginning. But in at least one way I'm certain of my reactions—I love you! I wish I could see you an hour to tell you how much!

Three weeks earlier, Churchill, in a meeting with Eisenhower and the British Chiefs of Staff on Malta, told Ike that since Marshall would be appointed to head the invasion of Europe, Overlord, that it was reasonable that a British General be the ground commander. This left Eisenhower with the likelihood of returning to Washington as Army Chief of Staff. He wanted, instead, to remain under Marshall and to command an Army in the war zone.

Two days after writing this letter, Eisenhower was riding in a car with Roosevelt after the Tehran Conference, when FDR told

General Dwight D. Eisenhower, handwritten and signed letter.

be different from what he was at the
beginning. But in at least one way I'm
certain of my reaction — I love you!
I wish I could see you an hour to tell
you how much!

Yesterday I sent a note to Johny —
I truly like to get his letters. This time
he sent me a couple of sketches.

Well darling — I must hop along. These
past few weeks have been hectic & much
of my preoccupation has been on things not
strictly my business. This kind of thing
always gets me irritated. Remember me to
friends — and lots & lots of love to you.
            Always — Ike.

    P.S. Mickey is under the weather for
    a couple of days and I'm sunk! I can
    scarcely find the things for dressing
    in the mornings. When I start on
    a trip it's terrible! But he'll be
    back in 2 days.

    Happy Christmas & New Year!!!
                        N

XXIX

The Medal of Honor Awarded to the Navy's Greatest Ace, With 34 Aerial Victories Over Japanese Planes in Combat

On June 19 and 20, 1944, the Battle of the Philippine Sea took place during the American invasion of the Mariana Islands. With American forces landing on Saipan, Japan jockeyed for a critical naval battle, with both their carrier and land-based aircraft playing the decisive role. On the first day, David McCampbell shot down seven dive bombers, in a one-sided air battle that would be immortalized in the phrase *"Marianas Turkey Shoot."*

Four months later, on October 24, 1944, American forces were landing in the Philippines and the Japanese again tried for what was now a desperate attempt to destroy the American Navy. They mobilized nearly all their remaining major ships to defeat the invasion in the Battle of Leyte Gulf. McCampbell shot down a record nine Japanese planes in one day.

He became the only person to twice become a Fighter Pilot Ace in one day. He had previously been awarded the Navy Cross, the Silver Star, the Legion of Merit with Combat V, three Distinguished Flying Crosses, and the Air Medal.

THE WHITE HOUSE
WASHINGTON

The President of the United States takes pleasure in presenting the MEDAL OF HONOR to

COMMANDER DAVID MC CAMPBELL, UNITED STATES NAVY

for service as set forth in the following

CITATION:

"For conspicuous gallantry and intrepidity at the risk of his life above and beyond the call of duty as Commander, Air Group FIFTEEN during combat against enemy Japanese aerial forces in the First and Second Battles of the Philippine Sea. An inspiring leader, fighting boldly in the face of terrific odds, Commander McCampbell led his fighter planes against a force of eighty Japanese carrier-based aircraft bearing down on our Fleet on June 19, 1944. Striking fiercely in valiant defense of our surface force, he personally destroyed seven hostile planes during this single engagement in which the outnumbering attack force was utterly routed and virtually annihilated. During a major Fleet engagement with the enemy on October 24, Commander McCampbell, assisted by but one plane, intercepted and daringly attacked a formation of sixty hostile land-based craft approaching our forces. Fighting desperately but with superb skill against such overwhelming air power, he shot down nine Japanese planes and, completely disorganizing the enemy group, forced the remainder to abandon the attack before a single aircraft could reach the Fleet. His great personal valor and indomitable spirit of aggression under extremely perilous combat conditions reflect the highest credit upon Commander McCampbell and the United States Naval Service."

Franklin D. Roosevelt

President Franklin Delano Roosevelt, typewritten and signed official document.

Commander David McCampbell in the cockpit, with 30 "kills" marked on the side of his plane.

XXX

Churchill to Stalin,
Deciding the Fate of Poland
October 15, 1944

> *"What we think . . . may prove a solution of our Polish troubles."*

Churchill's draft memorandum to Stalin, Moscow, October 15, 1944, was written while he was in Moscow to negotiate with Stalin over the future of European countries. Churchill proposed a list of "spheres of interest" in eastern and southern Europe, between Russia on one side and Britain and the Americans on the other. Churchill and Stalin were in agreement except over the question of Poland, in part because there were rival Polish governments-in-exile—one set up by Russia and the other supported by England. The issue of the Polish/Russian border was also subject to negotiation.

The ultimate disposition of Poland, under Russia's control, was not finally resolved until the Yalta Conference in February, 1945.

Churchill, Roosevelt, and Stalin at the Yalta Conference

19. Downing Street.
Whitehall.
Moscow.

October 15, 1944.

My dear Marshal Stalin,

Eden, by toiling through the best part of the night, has got what we think may prove a solution of is a satisfactory and reasonable formula from the Poles. Let me know when it would be convenient for me and Eden to bring this to you. We hope Molotov will be with you, and are at your service at any time. I remain,

With sincere respect.

Winston S. Churchill

Marshal Stalin.

Prime Minister Winston Churchill, signed official document (annotated).

XXXI

Eisenhower Writes to His Wife
April 16, 1944

"It is a terribly sad business. . . . to realize how many youngsters are gone forever."

Sweetheart . . . How I wish this cruel business of war could be completed quickly. . . . It is a terribly sad business to tot up the casualties each day—even in an air war—and to realize how many youngsters are gone forever. A man must develop a veneer of callousness that lets him consider such things dispassionately, but he can never escape a recognition of the fact that back home the news brings anguish and suffering to families all over the country. Mothers, fathers, brothers, sisters, wives and friends must have a difficult time preserving any comforting philosophy and retaining any belief in the eternal righteousness of things. War demands great toughness of fibre—not only in the soldier that must endure, but in the home that must sacrifice their best.

Eisenhower at this time was in London completing plans for Overlord, the invasion of France, on June 6.

General Dwight D. Eisenhower, handwritten and signed letter.

Eisenhower reviews the troops before the Normandy invasion.

How I wish this cruel business of war could be completed quickly. Entirely aside from my longing to return to you (and stay there) it is a terribly sad business to list up the casualties each day — even in an air war — and to realize how many youngsters are gone forever. A man must develop a veneer of callousness that lets him consider such things dispassionately; but he can never escape a recognition of the fact that back home its news brings anguish and suffering to families all over the country. Mothers, fathers, brothers, sisters, wives and friends must have a difficult time preserving any comforting philosophy and retaining any belief in the eternal rightness of things. War demands real toughness of fiber — not only in the soldier that must endure, but in the homes that must sacrifice their best.

We are very busy — which is fortunate, I suppose. But every once in a while I do get a evening for a week's leave. Just to go to sleep in the sun (but

I'd have to go somewhere else to find it.)

But I look forward to the day when we can travel and loaf together (maybe the docs will let you fly). I'd like to go to the corners of the Earth — maybe writing enough to keep us going — but without schedule and with no regard for time. It would be fun to see Bagdad, Rangoon, Sydney, Tahiti, Quito, Brazzaville and Timbuktu. I'd like also to travel throughout Russia. Would you?

Well my darling — the time for my first appointment for the day is here. I love you deeply, all the time, and miss you so much.

always.

Ike

P.S. My best to the folks and to all our San Antonio friends.

XXXII

The Original Map With Blue-and-Red Manuscript Markings Specifying the First Division Will Land at Omaha Beach and Its Objectives at First Light of the Second Day— Part of the Very Extensive and Detailed Invasion Plans

The Second Front, the invasion of Europe, had been the dominating issue between England and the United States since America entered the war. The United States wanted a plan and date from the beginning, but Churchill knew the Allies couldn't be ready for years. North Africa, he argued, was much more realistic; Roosevelt wouldn't agree with Churchill's view on timing. The United States, FDR believed, needed to "do something" in Europe to maintain the European focus of the people; otherwise they would turn to the Pacific and Japan.

When Russia entered the war after the German invasion in June 1942, Stalin strenuously argued for an immediate Second Front to draw German troops from the Russian Front. Meetings of the three leaders focused primarily on this contentious issue, with Stalin arguing that Russia was doing all the fighting while Britain and the United States were concentrating on North Africa and then Italy.

On July 15, 1943, Lt. General Frank Morgan presented a very detailed assessment of whether the Allies could invade France, where it could be done and when. The beaches of Normandy were the most likely to be successful, and May 1944 was the target date.

June 6, 1944, became D-Day. One hundred seventy-five thousand Allied troops would land on D-Day along with 50,000 vehicles; 5,333 ships would be in the armada from English Channel ports; 11,000 airplanes would fly 14,600 sorties on that fateful day; 2,000,000 men would eventually land in France.

It was the day that changed the history of Europe. It was the day that changed the course of World War II. It will forever be D-Day.

General Eisenhower speaks to 1st Lieutenant Wallace Strobel and other troops of the
101st Airborne on the eve of the D-Day invasion.

Eisenhower's Printed Message Given to Each Member of the Invasion Force, Autographed by Him for a Soldier
June 6, 1944

Dwight Eisenhower's message on D-Day was broadcast on board every troop ship heading to the beaches of Normandy. This printed copy of his memorable and inspiring words was one of tens of thousands distributed to every person on D-Day. It is one of the only ones distributed that day that he personally signed.

"You are about to embark upon the Great Crusade."

SUPREME HEADQUARTERS
ALLIED EXPEDITIONARY FORCE

Soldiers, Sailors and Airmen of the Allied Expeditionary Force!

You are about to embark upon the Great Crusade, toward which we have striven these many months. The eyes of the world are upon you. The hopes and prayers of liberty-loving people everywhere march with you. In company with our brave Allies and brothers-in-arms on other Fronts, you will bring about the destruction of the German war machine, the elimination of Nazi tyranny over the oppressed peoples of Europe, and security for ourselves in a free world.

Your task will not be an easy one. Your enemy is well trained, well equipped and battle-hardened. He will fight savagely.

But this is the year 1944! Much has happened since the Nazi triumphs of 1940-41. The United Nations have inflicted upon the Germans great defeats, in open battle, man-to-man. Our air offensive has seriously reduced their strength in the air and their capacity to wage war on the ground. Our Home Fronts have given us an overwhelming superiority in weapons and munitions of war, and placed at our disposal great reserves of trained fighting men. The tide has turned! The free men of the world are marching together to Victory!

I have full confidence in your courage, devotion to duty and skill in battle. We will accept nothing less than full Victory!

Good Luck! And let us all beseech the blessing of Almighty God upon this great and noble undertaking.

Dwight D Eisenhower

Eisenhower's Communiqué No. 1
Announcing the D-Day Landings
June 6, 1944

This carbon-copy typescript signed by Dwight Eisenhower was given to the British press corps at first light on D-Day. It was the announcement the world was waiting for—the opening of the Second Front, the invasion and liberation of Europe.

It was an announcement Hitler didn't believe when he woke up that afternoon. He was convinced the Allies would invade at the Pas de Calais, the closest point to England. Knowing through the breaking and reading of the German coded messages that this was Hitler's belief, an elaborate plan was created to convince Hitler that his intuition was correct. A completely fictitious army group was created with inflatable rubber tanks, fake airplanes, and other equipment that would convince German aerial reconnaissance experts; radio traffic commensurate with an army of hundreds of thousands of men and reports from German agents (actually British agents) all fed one of the greatest hoaxes ever created. George Patton was the commander of this army group; the Germans feared Patton as the best Allied commander, and as long as Patton was still in England, Hitler was convinced the Normandy landings were only a feint to lure the Germans from the real target—the Pas de Calais.

General Eisenhower, signed carbon-copy typescript.

XXXIII

The Two Commanders on Either Side of the English Channel Three Days After the Landings:
Dwight Eisenhower to His Wife
June 9, 1944

"My darling,

"... Anyway, we've started. Only time will tell how great our success will be. But all that can be done by human effort, intense devotion to duty, and courageous execution, all by thousands and thousands of individuals, will be done by this force. The soldiers, sailors and airmen are indescribable in their elan, courage, determination and fortitude. They inspire me."

General Eisenhower confers with Field Marshal Montgomery in an unknown location after Allied forces storm the Normandy beaches.

General Dwight D. Eisenhower, handwritten and signed letter.

Erwin Rommel to His Wife
June 9, 1944

"A lot of hardship has been our lot since our parting, and how much more hardship may still come? We are doing what we can, but the enemies' superiority in nearly all regards is overwhelming."

Field Marshal Rommel talks with an officer during the Allied landings.

Field Marshal Erwin Rommel, handwritten and signed postcard.

XXXIV

Charles de Gaulle Expresses His Strong Support for the French Resistance in a Speech Delivered in Algiers
November 3, 1943

General de Gaulle delivers an address in Algiers, November 16, 1943.

The French resistance. . . . that is how the immense masses of the nation have acted since June 18, 1940 as the very basis of the French war; our war is one and indivisible, whether it goes forward in the empire and on the battlefields abroad or in the interior of the battlefields at home.

The importance of Charles de Gaulle in restoring France's self-respect and position in postwar Europe cannot be overstated. He alone preserved the idea, unrealistic though it was, that France, as he said in his famous speech the day France surrendered, "has lost the battle but not the war." De Gaulle had been very prophetic in his 1934 article *"On the Army of the Future"* that Germany would simply drive around fixed fortifications, specifically France's Maginot Line. His belief that France should die fighting in the streets of Paris would have meant that France would not have had the future he was so responsible for. De Gaulle's statements about the French Resistance in this speech were greatly exaggerated, but it was what his country needed to hear, and he brought badly needed self-redemption for the badly defeated French Nation of 1940 and the necessarily collaborationist Vichy Government.

General Charles de Gaulle, typewritten and annotated document.

XXXV

Claus von Stauffenberg, the Leader of the July 20, 1944, Assassination Attempt to Kill Hitler, Writes From the Hospital After Being Badly Wounded in 1943

Stauffenberg's car was strafed in North Africa on April 7, 1943, and he spent three months in the hospital recovering from the loss of his right hand, two fingers from his left hand, and his left eye. When he signed this letter on May 19, 1943, five weeks later, it was with his crippled left hand, as his drawn and shaky signature shows.

Stauffenberg was the original organizer and leader of the plot to assassinate Hitler. His reasons were that Hitler was not conducting the war with military standards and rationale, and that elements of the military had become corrupt. He wanted to reestablish sound military rule and operations.

His fellow conspirator, General Helmuth Stieff, who also had personal access to Hitler in meetings, was originally to assassinate Hitler by shooting him, but backed out. Stauffenberg then took on the responsibility of both killing Hitler and organizing the military into a post-Hitler regime. Stauffenberg had wanted to set off a bomb at a meeting with Hitler, Goering, and Himmler present, but the opportunity did not occur, so he planned to set off a bomb at a meeting at Hitler's eastern headquarters at the Wolfsschanze on July 20, 1944. He placed his briefcase with the bomb under the conference table near Hitler and then excused himself and left the room. A few minutes later an aide moved the briefcase a few feet, enough that Hitler was only slightly injured.

Stauffenberg believed Hitler had been killed in the blast and flew to Berlin to initiate the second phase—the military takeover of the Third Reich. Goebbels, however, was broadcasting on the radio that Hitler had survived, and the central conspirators were quickly rounded up. Stauffenberg, along with others, was executed on July 21, 1944. The purge of those not fanatically supporting Hitler had just barely begun.

Claus von Stauffenberg, handwritten and signed postcard to Elisabeth von Schureppenburg: "I am very touched that you thought of me with such sympathy."

Sophie Scholl, a Student at Munich University, Created With Several Other Students the "White Rose Resistance" and Issued Leaflets Condemning the Nazis. She Was Betrayed and Guillotined the Same Day, February 22, 1943

Dissent within Germany was ruthlessly dealt with. Ministers who preached criticism of the Nazi regime from their pulpits were in concentration camps by the following Sunday. Others just disappeared. Sophie Scholl and her brother Hans were students in Munich who created the *White Rose* resistance. They wrote several leaflets criticizing the Nazis, which they anonymously placed around the university; they were betrayed, brought before a court, and executed by guillotine the same day.

Sophie School's university subject enrollment card, filled out and signed by her, 1942.

XXXVI

MacArthur Announces He Has Returned to the Philippines, and Tells the Filipino People How to Support the American Landings

October 20, 1944

Douglas MacArthur was one of the most enigmatic characters of World War II. He was recalled to the Army in July 1941 from the job he had taken as Field Marshall of the Army of the Philippines (Eisenhower told him it was pompous and ridiculous to call himself a field marshal of a virtually nonexistent army). He was Commander of the Army in the Far East, based in Manila, on December 8, 1941. He had been aware, in detail, of the Japanese attack on Pearl Harbor for nine hours, but made almost no defensive plans.

When the Japanese attacked his forces in the Philippines, he was frozen, literally allowing his Army Air Force to be totally destroyed on the ground. It is one of the greatest mysteries of the war why he refused to issue any orders for his airplanes to take off. Without any air power, his army was forced to retreat, in less than a month, to the Bataan Peninsula, where his entire force was killed or captured. MacArthur had escaped by PT boat to Australia, where he planned his return to the Philippines.

On October 20, 1944, he issued this message to the people of the Philippines, and famously waded ashore in front of the cameras set up on the beach, and strode up to the microphone to announce he had returned to the country he had lost to the Japanese so unnecessarily.

General Douglas MacArthur, typewritten and signed letter.

active operations, I counsel a period of alertness and preparation - a period in which full advantage must be taken of favorable opportunities to strike decisive blows but in which premature or ill-considered action, if it be at the expense of needless loss of life, is to be avoided.

5. Above all, I call for unity among the people - that unity so essential to the development of maximum strength at this critical time. Let the depth of your patriotism and your love of freedom rise above all differences, factional quarrels, disputes and petty jealousies, that all patriots unflinchingly may march shoulder to shoulder toward a common destiny.

The duration of the campaign and the human suffering which inevitably follows in the wake of war will be determined, in large measure, by the extent of your support. May God strengthen you to meet this test.

DOUGLAS MacARTHUR.

- 2 -

MacArthur wades into the Philippines.

XXXVII

Patton Describes the Battle of the Bulge As It Is Happening
December 23, 1944

"I am still of the opinion that the Germans are less numerous than other people think, and I am certain that when I get through with them they will be very much less numerous."

Adolf Hitler's last inspired military action was in the Fall of 1944. As the Allied Armies advanced across France and the Low Countries, Hitler conceived the idea of a last-ditch, all-out surprise attack in the Ardennes, the same terrain through which he attacked in May 1940, opening World War II. The steep, narrow valleys and numerous rivers convinced England and France in 1940 that the Germans would never attempt an attack through this terrain into Belgium, so it was a complete surprise when they did. Hitler correctly assumed it would never occur to the Allies that he would do it again. By December 1944, the rapid pace of the Allied advance across Europe had strained Allied troops and supplies. With the natural obstacles of the Ardennes, new and worn-out troops were placed there.

George Patton could see the danger, even though no one else did, and when the great German counter-offensive opened on December 16, Patton's concern was borne out. Hitler's goal was to drive to the coast

HEADQUARTERS
THIRD UNITED STATES ARMY
OFFICE OF THE COMMANDING GENERAL
APO 403

23 December, 1944

My dear Geoff:

Your letter of December 11 just reached me. I am in full accord with your feelings concerning what has happened, and I have heard many people here remark, with regret, that you had not gotten the 5th Army as we all believed you should.

On quite excellent authority I was informed that Lucian was given three stars for the purpose of commanding the 9th Army, but that through a slip in the War Department G-1, Charlie Simpson was sent over and it was not thought expedient to replace him.

In the meantime, Gerow had been slated for the 15th Army but had not been given three stars, therefore Lucian was to get the 15th. However, it became apparent about that time that we had too many armies; so, since Lucian had been made and had to have an army, he got the 5th. It is my personal opinion that but for this mischance, you would have had it. However, you must remember that, "Who the Lord loveth he chastenth," and God knows, you and I have been chastened considerably!

I am sure that if we keep doing our stuff we will sooner or later get the reward which we merit, and I know no one who merits a reward more than you. I told General Eisenhower and General Bradley, and also General Marshall that I considered you the outstanding candidate for an army command, and I am sure that some day you will have one.

As you have probably seen by the papers, my more or less successful progress through the Siegfried Line was halted by the necessity of pulling some chestnuts out of the fire, so now I am attacking, with everything I can scrape together, the left flank of the German salient.

Lieutenant General George S. Patton, typewritten and signed letter.

- 2 -

I am still of the opinion that the Germans are less numerous than other people think, and I am certain that when I get through with them they will be very much less numerous.

I certainly wish I had you here to add to the galaxy of Corps Commanders of whom I now have four, one of which, Milliken, is a rank amateur, and possibly also just rank, but I am not sure yet.

It was necessary to put Hugh Gaffey in command of the 4th Armored where he is doing a fine job. I took Gay back as Chief of Staff, which position he should have always occupied--not that Gaffey wasn't a good Chief of Staff for he is, but he is a better commander.

If I don't get hurt badly tonight--and that is always a possibility when fighting Germans--we will probably crack them to-morrow.

For the first time in weeks, we have had good flying weather today and have profited by it. I had eleven groups of mediums, seven groups of fighter-bombers, one-third of the 8th Air Force, and about 500 RAF planes helping me. For the first time the Germans were up in considerable force and did quite a lot of bombing. They got some of our gas and ammunition, but not enough to hurt.

I am very glad that you have sufficient confidence and affection for me to write me the letter you did. I end by assuring you that I agree with everything you said, and in wishing you all the success and happiness which you so greatly merit.

With affectionate regards, I am,

Devotedly yours,

George.

G. S. PATTON, JR.

Major General Geoffrey Keyes
Headquarters II American Corps
APO 19
U. S. Army
Italy

P.S. Since we sent me this post and it is the one you wrote me about

and capture Antwerp, dividing the Allied Armies. In what was seen as the greatest maneuver of a commander in World War II, Patton turned his Third Army 90 degrees, in terrible snow, and attacked the southern flank of the German thrust on December 22, the day before he wrote this letter.

As he writes in this letter, the weather was clear for flying; Patton dropped supplies to the Americans surrounded at Bastogne that day, but fighting through German forces to relieve the Americans was a bitter and slow battle. It was all or nothing for the Germans—they had no reserves, and war production was finally reduced by bombing to the point where even Albert Speer could not revive it.

Patton's brilliant planning, and the extraordinary training and discipline of his Third Army, prevented the Germans from having a chance at a breakout. They were pushed back into Germany, in retreat—a retreat that ended up against the Russians coming from the East. The war was over in 17 weeks.

Troops of the 101st Airborne Division watch C-47s drop supplies to them, December 26, 1944.

Patton's Christmas Greeting to the Troops

Patton had this Christmas greeting delivered to every one of his troops during the Battle of the Bulge. The reverse contains his famous "weather prayer" asking God to give them good weather for flying.

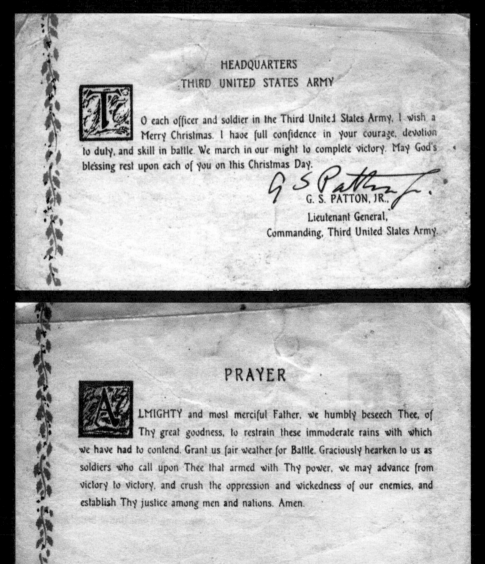

HEADQUARTERS
THIRD UNITED STATES ARMY

To each officer and soldier in the Third United States Army, I wish a Merry Christmas. I have full confidence in your courage, devotion to duty, and skill in battle. We march in our might to complete victory. May God's blessing rest upon each of you on this Christmas Day.

G. S. PATTON, JR.,
Lieutenant General,
Commanding, Third United States Army.

PRAYER

ALMIGHTY and most merciful Father, we humbly beseech Thee, of Thy great goodness, to restrain these immoderate rains with which we have had to contend. Grant us fair weather for Battle. Graciously hearken to us as soldiers who call upon Thee that armed with Thy power, we may advance from victory to victory, and crush the oppression and wickedness of our enemies, and establish Thy justice among men and nations. Amen.

Lieutenant General Patton, signed postcard.

XXXVIII

Mao Tse-Tung and Other Chinese Communist Leaders Attend a Christmas Eve Dinner, 1944, Given by Their American Advisors; the Typewritten Program List of Dinner Guests Is Autographed by the Communist Guerrilla Leaders

A group of approximately 20 Americans were sent as advisors to Mao Tse-Tung and his communist guerrilla force in China. The first Christmas was celebrated by the Americans with the Chinese. One of the guerrillas found a tree some distance away and brought it to the camp. The Christmas tree lights were flashlight bulbs hooked together, and weather balloons were decorated with "Merry Christmas" in Chinese characters painted on the sides. The Americans wrapped approximately 60 to 70 small gifts—bars of soap, tins of tobacco, cigarettes, tinned foods, and other things unobtainable to the Chinese. They gave each of the Americans a crock of *Hoo-Goo*—an alcoholic rum containing crushed bone, which the Chinese believe has curing powers. They also gave each of the Americans a doll dressed as a guerrilla woman holding a spear.

The Americans sang Christmas carols and the communists sang *lao-Bao-Chil*, songs of the working men.

Typewritten dinner program, signed by the guests named therein.

XXXIX

Anne Frank

"Margot and Anne were taken to Belsen as they were too weak to work. Margot got typhus and died and Anne who knew her mother was dead and felt sure her father must be dead also, just faded away." Alice Frank, Anne's paternal grandmother, September, 1945

Anne and Margot died, it is believed, in early 1945, just before Belsen was liberated by British troops.

Alice Frank-Stern, handwritten note, September 1945.

Alice Frank-Stern with her granddaughters Margot and Anne, July 21, 1929.

"Anne's book is very successful here and in November the second edition will come out. . . . I hope I can succeed in having English and German editions published." Otto Frank, Anne's father, the only member of the family to survive, October 14, 1947

Otto Frank, because he was able to work, was kept at Auschwitz, where he was liberated by the Soviets on January 27, 1945. He returned to Amsterdam where he searched for his family through 1945; he realized by the end of the year that he was the sole survivor.

Anne's diary had been rescued from the family's hiding place by Miep Gies, who gave it to her father; he left it unread until he transcribed it for relatives in Switzerland. It was first published on June 25, 1947, in Dutch, and as Otto Frank writes in this letter, it met great success. It was published in English in 1952.

Otto Frank remarried a fellow Holocaust survivor from Auschwitz and lived until 1980. He organized the Anne Frank Foundation to save the house where they hid in Amsterdam; it is open to the public.

Otto Frank, typewritten and signed letter, October 14, 1947.

Oscar Schindler, Who Saved Polish Jews by Putting Them on His "List" of Factory Workers

Oscar Schindler was a German industrialist and member of the Nazi Party who became one of the most famous humanitarians of World War II. He owned enamelware and ammunition factories in Poland and Czechoslovakia, and became so taken by the persecution of the Jews that he began employing them in large numbers, saving the lives of over 1,200 by declaring them critical to the war effort. Toward the end of the war he spent his fortune on bribes and the black market, helping them to survive. When his enamelware factory was to be closed as unnecessary for the war effort, and his workers sent to an extermination camp, he created a list of workers who were essential for a new factory in the Sudetenland to produce hand-grenades and V2 rocket parts. This list became the basis of a book about his humanitarian efforts, and of *Schindler's List*, an important movie.

After the war, his fortune spent in saving the Jews, Schindler wandered through various countries and back to Germany, impoverished. He died in 1974, age 66, penniless. He is buried, as he wished, in Jerusalem, with the highest honors of the State of Israel.

Raoul Wallenberg Signed Swedish Protective Passport for a Jew in Budapest
October 10, 1944

"Mrs. Kellner is to be considered a Swedish citizen and is to be exempted from bearing the distinctive Jewish sign." Raoul Wallenberg, the Swedish businessman who rescued Hungarian Jews

Raoul Wallenberg was a Swedish businessman and diplomat in Budapest who issued Swedish protective passports to tens of thousands of Hungarian Jews, saving them from deportation and death. He also declared many buildings part of the Swedish Embassy compound in order to shelter Jews. It is estimated he likely saved the lives of about 100,000 Hungarian Jews.

He died mysteriously in Soviet custody, probably about 1947.

KÖNIGLICH
SCHWEDISCHE GESANDTSCHAFT
BUDAPEST

A Külföldieket Ellenőrző Orsz. Közp. Hatóságnak,

Budapest.

Van szerencsénk közölni, hogy a budapesti Svéd Kir. Követség

Kellner Ferencné urnő

részére védőútlevelet állított ki, melynek értelmében nevezett svéd alattvalónak tekintendő.

Tisztelettel kéri a Követség, sziveskedjenek nevezettnek a megkülönböztető jelzés viselése alól való mentességet megadni. Igazolja a Követség, hogy a vonatkozó rendeletben emlitett viszonosság Svédországgal fennáll.

Budapest, 1944. okt.lo.

Kiváló tisztelettel

R.: 7813.

Sp.: 74/86

Svéd kir. követ helyett
Svéd kir. követségi titkár.

Raoul Wallenberg, signed official passport document, October 10, 1944.

XLI

Hitler's Signed Orders for the Fanatical Defense of Berlin Four Weeks Before His Suicide
March 30, 1945

On March 30, 1945, Hitler orders that the "German Army, from the Commander in Chief to the youngest man, be entirely aware that only the toughest will to resistance and fanatic determination can guarantee the success of the coming fight. Then the battle before Berlin must and will end with a decisive defensive victory." The document promises that "the forces liberated in east and west Prussia will arrive" later and gives specific orders to various units for the final defense of the German capital.

On this day the Third Reich was collapsing. American and British forces were advancing across Germany with lightning speed and the Russians were steadily advancing from the East with a ferocity that even the Germans found terrifying. Hitler was depending on his Army Group Vistula, the recipient of this order, to defend Berlin itself. Two days earlier Field Marshal Kesselring had told Hitler that the soldiers on the Western Front were surrendering, white flags were everywhere, and civilians were welcoming the Allied soldiers.

Joseph Goebbels, his most loyal and trusted ally, wrote in his diary about the desperate state of German morale and Hitler's refusal to address the country as the Third Reich was disintegrating. The Germans wanted to surrender to the Americans and British and were fleeing ahead of the Soviet onslaught.

Adolf Hitler, Führer of the German Reich, signed official order, March 30, 1945.

Hitler himself was disintegrating. Ten days earlier he had issued his order that all German industry, buildings, railways, and bridges were to be destroyed. Albert Speer, Minister of Armaments and Production, was fired for opposing the order, which Hitler had reaffirmed March 27 with even stronger language about destroying all material wealth in Germany. Realizing his need for Speer's cooperation, he summoned him to Berlin, and Speer managed to convince Hitler to put him in charge of carrying out this order. He knew Speer wouldn't do it, but Hitler's delusions on March 30 were swinging the other way, as this document attests. Instead of fanatical destruction, Hitler now demanded the fanatical defense of his capitol city, promising troops from the Eastern Front, when that was where Germany was most threatened as the Soviet Army was doing to Germany what they had done to Russia, destroying and killing everything.

Hitler always saw himself as characters from Richard Wagner's operas. In the early 1930s he had his portrait painted as Lohengrin riding to the rescue of Germany. Now he was in the final act of Wagner's *Götterdämmerung*—the fires of complete destruction.

- 2 -

326

Im einzelnen befehle ich:

1) Die H.Gr. gliedert sich unter Einsatz bisher noch zurückgehaltener Verbände in der Front so zur Abwehr, daß bei jedem Divisionsabschnitt eine genügende Tiefe erreicht wird.

2) Etwa 3 - 6 km hinter den jetzigen HKL ist eine Großkampf-HKL zu bestimmen und auszubauen, deren rechtzeitiges Beziehen der Oberbefehlshaber der Heeresgruppe bei erkanntem unmittelbaren Bevorstehen des fdl. Grossangriffs anzuordnen hat. Auf keinen Fall darf die zu erwartende Artillerie-Massenwirkung des Gegners unsere gesamte Verteidigung zerschlagen.

3) Das beschleunigte Einrücken der Ausbildungsverbände des Ersatzheeres und der Luftwaffe in die rückwärtige 8 - 1o km hinter der HKL verlaufende Stelle ist mit aller Energie zu erzwingen.

4) Die Artillerie ist schon jetzt so in die Tiefe zu gliedern, daß die Mehrzahl der Batterien noch Sperrfeuer vor jetzige HKL abzugeben in der Lage ist, aber nur wenige Batterien im dauernden Wechsel für Fernaufgaben vorgezogen bleiben. Einzelne Batterien müssen sich in der Linie der Ausbildungsverbände befinden.

5) Nach Abgabe der 1o.SS-Pz.Div. an die H.Gr.Mitte sind alle schnellen Verbände als Eingreifreserven heranzuziehen und so hinter den wahrscheinlichen

-3-

- 3 -   325

Hauptangriffsabschnitten des Gegners bereitzuhalten,
daß sie unverzüglich zum Gegenangriff vorgeführt
werden können. Ihre ständige Einsatzbereitschaft ist
durch häufige Übungen zu überprüfen.

6) Die beabsichtige Gliederung im einzelnen für die Ab-
wehrschlacht ist zum 1.4. zu melden.

Der Führer.

OKH/GenStdH/Op Abt (roem.1a)
Nr.   /45 g.Kdos.Chefs.

XLII

Five Days Before His Death and Four Months Before Hiroshima, Franklin Roosevelt Writes of "Complete Victory Over Our Enemies"
April 9, 1945

When Franklin D. Roosevelt wrote this letter he had every reason to be confident about the war and the "complete victory over our enemies."

Eight days earlier, American forces had invaded Okinawa with unexpectedly light opposition (that was about to change violently). The Japanese knew that Okinawa would be the last battle before an invasion of the mainland, 300 miles away, and that Okinawa would be the staging and supply base for the final invasion.

In Germany, the American troops were far into the German heartland, advancing almost at will, and the Russians were poised to launch the final assault on Berlin one week later. Their 2,500,000 men were supported by 6,250 tanks, 7,500 planes, and 41,600 artillery. The losses in the street-by-street, house-by-house fighting were without quarter, and hundreds of thousands of men on both sides were lost before there was no longer a German opposition left to fight in Berlin.

THE WHITE HOUSE
WASHINGTON

April 9, 1945

Dear Bishop Oxnam:

I wish you Godspeed as you take off on a dual mission, in some respects of unique interest.

A common patriotism and a determination to win the war, foremost in all American hearts, have brought all of our citizens into closer union. Without regard to religious affiliations or individual loyalties, we and our allies have worked together to achieve complete victory over our enemies. It is therefore of happy significance that you, as President of The Federal Council of the Churches of Christ in America, are journeying to an ancient English city to represent that very inclusive body of American Christians at the enthronement of the Archbishop of Canterbury. I think that is an exemplification of the spirit which should bind together Christians of all nations and loyalties in the bonds of fellowship and good will.

Permit me also to wish you success as you continue your travels as representative of the General Commission on Army and Navy Chaplains to visit the chaplains in the Mediterranean theater of operations. That visitation will bear witness to the importance which we place on spiritual things and will, I trust, strengthen alike the morale of our chaplains and the forces to whom they minister.

Very sincerely yours,

Franklin Roosevelt

Bishop G. Bromley Oxnam, D.D.,
President,
The Federal Council of the
   Churches of Christ in America,
150 Fifth Avenue,
New York 11, N. Y.

President Roosevelt, photographed four days after writing this letter.

XLIII

The Russian Troops' Statement Read When Meeting the Americans at the Elbe River, Near Torgau, Germany
April 25, 1945

The meeting of American troops coming from the west and Soviet troops coming from the east was not uncomplicated. The German Army was between the advancing forces, and great care and thought had to go into preventing the two armies from shelling each other with artillery or accidently firing at each other with small arms and mortars.

The link-up was accomplished when reconnaissance patrols encountered each other; the Soviets were prepared with this message to be read to the Americans. The joining of forces at Torgau, between Leipzig and Dresden, cut Germany in two and was the last major event before the fall of Berlin.

My dearest friends!

To day is a great holiday. We are sitting with officers and soldiers which have freeded us from the Germans. For us iki ix it is a clark memory when we remember the time of the Naziregime when we think of how many have died. These dead we shall never forget. Some of You were the first to come to this town and have brought us freedom. The alied army have on all fronts, the americans in Africa and Evrope and the Russians from Stalingrad destr the German Enemy. Fashism and National socialism are dead forever.

I wish all of you helth and good luck.

Long live your president of the U.S.A. Mr.Truman and our Marshal Stalin.

Mai dir frends!

Tu dei is e greit holidei. Wi ar sitting wis oficers end doldjers witsch hev fridid as from se djermens. For as it is x e klark memori wen wi rimember i se teim of se Naziredjim, wen wi sink of hau meny hew deid. Sis ded wi schel never forget. Sam of ju wer se i ferst tu cam tu sis taun end haw brod as fridom. Se aleid army hew on ol fronts, si amerikein in afrika se raschien from Stalingrad se germen enmi.

Ei wisch ju all hels end gud lack.

Long liw jaur president of se juneitid stets Trumen end aur marschal Stalin.

Typescript of speech delivered April 25, 1945.

Russian and U.S. soldiers meet at the Elbe.

XLIV

Eisenhower Announces Germany's Surrender to George Patton
May 7, 1945

Admiral Karl Donitz, as Hitler's designated successor as Führer, attempted to negotiate with Eisenhower over the surrender of Germany. Donitz sent General Alfred Jodl, the Chief of Staff of the German Armed Forces High Command, to Reims, where Eisenhower had established his headquarters. Eisenhower, who would not personally meet with any of the Nazi leaders, informed Jodl that his terms were unconditional surrender, and if not immediately accepted he would close his military lines to German soldiers, forcing them to surrender to the Soviets. Donitz had no choice, and Jodl signed the surrender of all German forces in the early hours of May 7, 1945.

CONFIDENTIAL   CONFIDENTIAL

SHAEF

STAFF MESSAGE CONTROL
OUTGOING MESSAGE

CONFIDENTIAL
URGENT
RECD IN CODE

TO   :THE COMMANDING GENERAL 3RD U.S. ARMY

FROM   :SHAEF FORWARD, SIGNED EISENHOWER

1. A representative of the German High Command signed the
    unconditional surrender of all German land, sea and air
    forces in Europe to the Allied expeditionary force
    at 0141 hours Central European time, 7 May 1945.

2. Effective immediately all offensive operations by Allied
    expeditionary force will cease. Full defensive precautions
    will be taken.

3. No release will be made to the press pending announcement
    by the heads of the three governments.

ORIGINATOR   :SUPREME COMMANDER

INFORMATION   :TO ALL GENERAL AND SPECIAL STAFF DIVISION

DWIGHT D. EISENHOWER
SUPREME COMMANDER OF ALLIED FORCES
7 May 1945

CONFIDENTIAL

General Dwight D. Eisenhower, typewritten and signed document, May 7, 1945.

XLV

Patton's Farewell to His Third Army
May 9, 1945

George Patton's heartfelt and sincere message to the Third Army two days after the German surrender masked his own despair that the war in Europe had ended, and that he might not be able to get a command in the Pacific. Forty-one years earlier he had written to his father upon being admitted to West Point about his fear that there wouldn't be any more wars for him to fight (number 19 in this book). He often said that he wanted to die from the last bullet fired in the war, and when an automobile accident struck him down later in 1945, he accepted the end quietly and with resignation. He was not a man for peace.

General George Patton's homecoming at the end of the war.

HEADQUARTERS
THIRD UNITED STATES ARMY
OFFICE OF THE COMMANDING GENERAL
APO 403

GENERAL ORDERS   9 May 1945

NUMBER 98

SOLDIERS OF THE THIRD ARMY, PAST AND PRESENT

During the 281 days of incessant and victorious combat, your penetrations have advanced farther in less time than any other army in history. You have fought your way across 24 major rivers and innumerable lesser streams. You have liberated or conquered more than 82,000 square miles of territory, including 1500 cities and towns, and some 12,000 inhabited places. Prior to the termination of active hostilities, you had captured in battle 956,000 enemy soldiers and killed or wounded at least 500,000 others. France, Belgium, Luxembourg, Germany, Austria, and Czechoslovakia bear witness to your exploits.

All men and women of the six corps and thirty-nine divisions that have at different times been members of this Army have done their duty. Each deserves credit. The enduring valor of the combat troops has been paralleled and made possible by the often unpublicized activities of the supply, administrative, and medical services of this Army and of the Communications Zone troops supporting it. Nor should we forget our comrades of the other armies and of the Air Force, particularly of the XIX Tactical Air Command, by whose side or under whose wings we have had the honor to fight.

In proudly contemplating our achievements, let us never forget our heroic dead whose graves mark the course of our victorious advances, nor our wounded whose sacrifices aided so much to our success.

I should be both ungrateful and wanting in candor if I failed to acknowledge the debt we owe to our Chiefs of Staff, Generals Gaffey and Gay, and to the officers and men of the General and Special Staff Sections of Army Headquarters. Without their loyalty, intelligence, and unremitting labors, success would have been impossible.

The termination of fighting in Europe does not remove the opportunities for other outstanding and equally difficult achievements in the days which are to come. In some ways the immediate future will demand of you more fortitude than has the past because, without the inspiration of combat, you must maintain -- by your dress, deportment, and efficiency -- not only the prestige of the Third Army but also the honor of the United States. I have complete confidence that you will not fail.

During the course of this war I have received promotions and decorations far above and beyond my individual merit. You won them; I as your representative wear them. The one honor which is mine and mine alone is that of having commanded such an incomparable group of Americans, the record of whose fortitude, audacity, and valor will endure as long as history lasts.

G. S. PATTON, JR.,
General.

General George S. Patton, typewritten and signed letter, May 9, 1945.

XLVI

The Operations Order That Launched the Atomic Age
August 6, 1945

Paul Tibbetts commanded the *Enola Gay* carrying the first atomic bomb; Charles Sweeney, the instrument plane; and George Marquardt, the photo plane. The fourth combat plane went ahead to Iwo Jima, in case of mechanical failure on the *Enola Gay*. The *Enola Gay*, number 82, carried 400 less gallons of fuel due to the 9,000-pound weight of the atomic bomb.

This operations order was carried on the *Enola Gay* in the flight log of Jacob Beser, the radar and electronics specialist trained to intercept any Japanese radar impulses that could trigger the special radar-operated fusing switch built into the atomic bomb. Beser has penciled "Hiroshima" in the lower right.

Colonel Paul W. Tibbets, the commander (at center, in jumpsuit), and the ground crew of the *Enola Gay*.

509TH COMPOSITE GROUP
Office of the Operations Officer
APO 247, c/o Postmaster
San Francisco, California

5 August 1945

OPERATIONS ORDER)

NUMBER   35)

Date of Mission: 6 August 1945

Briefings: : See below

Take-off: Weather Ships at 0200 (Approx)
           Strike Ships at 0300 (Approx)

Out of Sacks: Weather at 2230
               Strike at 2330

Mess   : 2315 to 0115

Lunches   : 39 at 2330
              52 at 0030

Trucks   : 3 at 0015
              4 at 0115

A/C NO.	VICTOR NO.	APCO	CREW SUBS	PASSENGERS (To Follow)
Weather Mission:				
298	83	Taylor		
303	71	Wilson		
301	85	Eatherly		
302	72	Alternate A/C		
Combat Strike:				
292	82	Tibbets	As Briefed	
353	89	Sweeney		
291	91	Marquardt		
354	90	McKnight		
304	88	Alternate for Marquardt		

GAS: #82 - 7000 gals.
      all others - 7400 gals.

AMMUNITION: 1000 rds/gun in all A/C.

BOMBS: Special.

CAMERAS: K18 in #82 and #90. Other installations per verbal orders.

RELIGIOUS SERVICES: Catholic at 2200
                     Protestant at 2230

BRIEFINGS:

Weather Ships
   General Briefing in Combat Crew Lounge at 2300.
   Special Briefings at 2330 as follows:
      AC and Pilots in Combat Crew Lounge
      Nav - Radar Operators in Library
      Radio Operators in Communications
      Flight Engineers in Operations
   Mess at 2330
   Trucks at 0015

Strike Mission:
   General Briefing in Combat Crew Lounge at 2400
   Special Briefings at 0030 as follows:
      AC and Pilots in Combat Crew Lounge
      Nav and Radar Operators in Library
      Radio Operators at Communications
      Flight Engineers at Operations
   Mess at 0030
   Trucks at 0115   NOTE: Lt McKnight's crew need not attend briefings.

JAMES I. HOPKINS, JR,
Major, Air Corps,
Operations Officer.

The detailed order for the atomic bomb attack on Hiroshima: *"BOMBS: Special."*

The Nagasaki Atomic Bomb
August 8, 1945

Charles Sweeney, commander of the instrument plane at Hiroshima, commanded the *Bock's Car* carrying the atomic bomb dropped on Nagasaki. Jacob Beser, the radar and electronics specialist on the Hiroshima raid, was the only person who flew in both planes dropping atomic bombs; he fulfilled the same role on the second mission. This operation order was carried by him on the Nagasaki raid; he penciled in "Nagasaki" in the lower left.

Major Charles Sweeney, the commander (fifth from right), and the crew of the *Bock's Car*, two days after the Nagasaki mission.

```
                    408TH COMPOSITE GROUP
                    Office of the Operations Officer
                    APO 336, c/o Postmaster
                    San Francisco, California

                                              8 August 1945
OPERATIONS ORDER)
            :
NUMBER      39)                    Out of Sacks: Weather 2300
                                                 Strike 2400
Date of Mission: 9 August 1945

Briefings:  See Below             Mess: 2345 to 0145

Take-off: Weather ships: 0230     Lunches: 24 at 2400
          Strike Ships: 0330               48 at 0100

ETA:  1630                         Trucks: 2 at 0045
                                           4 at 0145

  A/C NO.      VICTOR NO.    APCO      CREW SUBS       PASSENGERS

 Weather Mission:
    398          82         Marquardt
    347          95         McKnight

 Combat Strike:
    297          77         Sweeney                    Beser
    353          89         Bock
    354          90         Hopkins (Crew C-14)

 To Iwo
    298          83         Taylor                     Col Smith
                                                       T/Sgt Kupfenberg

 Alternates for above aircraft:
    291          91         1st Alternate
    301          85         2nd Alternate

GAS: A/C #77  7250                AMMUNITION: 1000 rds per gun.
     All others 7400

BOMBS: Special                    CAMERAS: K-20 in all strike A/C & Alternates

RELIGIOUS SERVICES: Catholic:  1830
                    Protestant: 2300

BRIEFINGS:

    Weather Ships
    General briefing in War Room at 2330
    Special briefings immediately following General as follows:
        A/C and P - Operations
        Nav. and Rad Oprs. - War Room.
        Bombardiers - War Room.
        Flt Engs - Library.

    Strike Ships
    General briefing in War Room at 0030.
    Special briefings immediately following General as follows:
        A/C and P - Operations.
        Nav and Rad Opr. - War Room.
        Bombardiers - War Room.
        Flt Engs. - Library.

    All Radio Operators brief in Communications at 2230.

Nagasaki                               James I Hopkins Jr.
                                       JAMES I HOPKINS JR,
                                       Major, Air Corps,
                                       Operations Officer.
```

Operations order, August 8, 1945.

XLVII

MacArthur's Draft of the Japanese Surrender Terms
August 1945

Douglas MacArthur's surrender terms for Japan were prepared by him as Supreme Commander for the Allied Powers. The second atomic bomb dropped on Nagasaki began to persuade some Japanese, notably Emperor Hirohito, that they needed to consider that the war had to end. Hirohito had refused, into July, to listen to any discussion of ending the war; he insisted on one more major victory. Given that only the Japanese homeland remained as a potential battleground, and that the navy and air force were completely destroyed, a victory could only come against an invasion force. The second atomic bomb, coming only days after Hiroshima, backed up Truman's statement that there would be an endless rain of atomic devastation.

During the six days after Nagasaki, on August 9, 1945, violent struggles went on within Japan's leadership over ending the war. Hirohito finally spoke on the radio (the first time the Japanese heard his voice) to declare an end to the war.

MacArthur ordered a Japanese delegation to fly on August 19, in two planes painted white with green crosses, to Okinawa, where they would be transferred to an American cargo plane and flown to Manila to be presented with this surrender document on August 20. He ordered that the Japanese planes use the code word "Bataan" to enter Okinawan air space. The Japanese responded that they would use "JNP." MacArthur stated that it must be "Bataan," and saw to it that their planes were challenged a dozen times by American fighter planes.

MacArthur then orchestrated the formal surrender aboard the Battleship *Missouri* in Tokyo Bay on September 2, 1945.

REQUIREMENTS
OF THE
SUPREME COMMANDER FOR THE ALLIED POWERS
PRESENTED TO JAPANESE REPRESENTATIVES
AT MANILA, P.I., 20 AUGUST 1945

III

REQUIREMENTS FOR ENTRY OF THE SUPREME COMMANDER FOR THE ALLIED POWERS AND HIS ACCOMPANYING FORCES

1. The Japanese Imperial Government and Japanese Imperial General Headquarters will require execution of the following requirements, effective 1800 hours 24 August 1945.

a. Japanese Armed Forces and civil aviation authorities will insure that all Japanese military, naval and civil aircraft in Japan remain on the ground, on the water or aboard ship until further notification of the disposition to be made of them.

b. Japanese or Japanese-controlled military, naval or merchant vessels of all types in Japanese waters will be maintained without damage and will undertake no movement beyond voyages in progress, pending instructions of the Supreme Commander for the Allied Powers. Vessels at sea will immediately render harmless and throw overboard explosives of all types. Vessels not at sea will immediately remove explosives of all types to safe storage ashore.

c. Merchant vessels under 100 gross tons engaged in civilian supply activities in Japanese waters are excepted from the foregoing instructions. Vessels in TOKYO BAY engaged in evacuation of personnel from the YOKOSUKA Naval Base are also excepted.

d. Japanese or Japanese-controlled ships at sea, wherever located, will report their positions in plain language immediately to the nearest United States, British or Soviet radio station on

- 1 -

General Douglas MacArthur, typewritten document, August 1945.

MacArthur's Statement
After the Japanese Surrender

"I shall at once take steps to end hostilities and stop unnecessary bloodshed."

I thank a merciful God that this mighty struggle is about to end. The magnificent men and women who have fought so nobly to victory can now return to their homes in due course and resume their civil pursuits. They have been good soldiers in war. May they be equally good citizens in peace.

General MacArthur, typescript of oral statement (annotated), no date.

General Douglas MacArthur (far left) observes as Admiral Chester W. Nimitz signs the Japanese surrender agreement on behalf of the United States.

German Mug Shots

DETENTION REPORT

I.C. — 1096-14-2-45. — 76456.

File number

SEX

(M) F

Ring applicable

Office use only

GOERING
HERMANN
31G 350013
22 JUNE 1945

Do not write in shaded portions

Surname : GOERING

First names : HERMANN

Aliases :

Civil Occupation : Regular Army Officer

Nationality : German   (2)

DATE OF BIRTH	(3)		PLACE OF BIRTH	(3a)		WEIGHT	(3b)	HEIGHT (4)
12 JAN 1893					ROSENHEIM, BAVARIA	118 k		1.78 m

DETENTION REPORT

File number

SEX (I)

M F

Ring applicable

Office use only

Surname : JODL

First names : ALFRED

Aliases :

Civil Occupation : Regular Army Officer

Nationality : German (2)

DATE OF BIRTH	(3)		PLACE OF BIRTH	(3a)		WEIGHT	(3b)	HEIGHT (4)
10 MAY 1890					WURZBURG	76 K		1.76 m

I.C. — 1096-14-2-45. — 76456.

JODL ALFRED 31G 350026 22 JUNE 1945

DETENTION REPORT

File number

SEX (I)

M F

Ring applicable

Office use only

Surname : KEITEL

First names : WILHELM

Aliases :

Civil Occupation : Regular Army

Nationality : German (2)

DATE OF BIRTH	(3)		PLACE OF BIRTH	(3a)		WEIGHT	(3b)	HEIGHT (4)
22 Sept. 1882				Kr. Gandersheim	Helmscherode	180 lbs.		1.85 m.

I.C. — 1096-14-2-45. — 76456.

KEITEL WILHELM 31G 350003 22 JUNE 1945

The Signatures of All the Imprisoned Nazi War-Trial Defendants at Nürnberg; Eleven Were Hanged and Three Acquitted, and Six Served 10 Years to Life

The surviving major Nazi figures were put on trial in Nürnberg for war crimes. All of them, except Albert Speer, defended themselves by saying they had only been following orders and had been unaware of atrocities. Speer testified that he also had been unaware of atrocities, but that he should have known, and deeply regretted his role in the Third Reich. Because of his recognition that he avoided knowing what was happening in the concentration camps, and his personal feelings of guilt, his life was spared and he was sentenced to 20 years' imprisonment. Ten others were hanged, Goering managed to commit suicide, three were acquitted, and five served between ten years and life. Rudolph Hess, perhaps the most controversial defendant (he wasn't in Germany during most of the war, having flown to England in 1941 on a misguided peace mission), died in prison at 93 years old.

It was expressly against the rules for the American guards at Nürnberg to collect autographs, but it was a common pursuit. The Nazis were very happy to oblige, restoring to them some sense of self-importance.

The Major Japanese War Criminals' Autographed Mug Shots in English

The war trials in Tokyo were controversial because the major force behind Japan's war was not on trial. Emperor Hirohito's very active role in the war, and particularly his refusal to consider ending the war in 1945 without a major victory on Japan's homeland, was covered up by the Americans in order to keep him as Japan's leader. The Americans feared that without the Emperor the Japanese people would be ungovernable.

The group of Japanese in this series of mug shot–like photographs were the "Class A" criminals. All were found guilty. Of the 26, seven were executed, one was found to be insane, 16 received life sentences, and two received lesser sentences. When the Americans ended the occupation in 1952 and turned the prisoners over to the Japanese, all of them were released.

The Japanese war criminals are enshrined in the Yasukuni Shrine in Tokyo (along with all those who served the Emperor in World War II). This honoring of those guilty of war-time atrocities continues to fuel outrage among the Asian countries, particularly China and Korea.

The Architect of Japan's War on the United States, on Trial for War Crimes, Requests an Image of Buddha, Rosary Beads, and a Photograph of His Children, Arguing These Are His Rights Under International Law and Treaties

Hideki Tojo was the most powerful person in Japan, except for Emperor Hirohito, in modern times. He was an active general in the Army and became Minister of the Army in 1940. In 1941 he became Prime Minister and was also, at the same time, Foreign Minister, Education Minister, Home Minister, Minister of the Army, and Chief of the Imperial Army. He ruled all aspects of Japanese life with an iron fist.

Tojo led the government in deciding to go to war in 1941. He launched the attack on Pearl Harbor, and conquered most of East and South East Asia. He was the face, and the name, of war-time Japan, given equal focus in Allied propaganda with Hitler and Mussolini. As the tide of war changed after the Japanese defeat on Saipan, opposition within the government, and most importantly from Emperor Hirohito, pushed him aside in 1944, but he remained influential.

During his trial for war crimes, including the barbaric treatment and executions of American prisoners, he strayed from the agreed-upon script of exonerating the Emperor of all involvement in the war and testified to Hirohito's direct involvement in Japan's decision to go to war. After a court recess, he recanted his testimony and it was stricken from the record. He was hanged later in 1948.

13 February 1948

FROM : Hideki TOJO

TO : Colonel Crary, Commanding Officer, Sugamo Prison

SUBJECT: Petition Concerning Personal Effects.

Request is respectfully made herein for the return of the following personal effects, which were removed from my compartment at Sugamo Prison on 12 February 1948:

1. A small sized hand book with an image of Buddha pasted thereon, and a passage of Sutra printed therein.

2. A string of beads (rosary) loaned or furnished by the Prison authorities.

3. A small sized photograph of children (family).

In support of my request permit me to make the following explanation:

The image of Buddha and passage of Sutra, as well as the beads, are indispensable for my daily religious worship, which is permitted in the prison as a universal interpretation of international law and treaties. Formerly the beads have been removed by prison guards but each time at my request were returned. I am a Buddist, as is known, and if my religious worship is to be suspended I desire a written order to that effect.

The photograph of the children is that of my very dearest ones, which I had hoped and do hope to have in my hands all through my lifetime, which is also their desires, as is written on the back thereof. As paternal love is the same in all nations I hope you will grant my request, which relates to a written order of 2 December 1946 signed by Major Augustin Swanson of the Prison wherein it was permitted that each prisoner be permitted one photograph. No change has been made in this order as I understand.

I sincerely request that you grant me the request contained herein.

Hideki TOJO

Hideki Tojo, typewritten and signed document, February 13, 1948.

XLIX

Truman Explains the Necessity of Dropping the Atomic Bomb
November 29, 1957

In the spring of 1945, the United States was making plans for the invasion of Japan. The first group would land on Kyushu on November 1 and the second group would land near Tokyo in mid-1946. Millions of men would be involved, and it was not at all clear that the American people would continue to support the Pacific War with the expected casualties. The Joint Chiefs of Staff estimated casualties at 1,200,000 men. There would not be enough Purple Hearts for the wounded and dead—500,000 more were minted (Purple Hearts being awarded today in Afghanistan were minted for the invasion of Japan in 1945).

The committee appointed to study the atomic bomb was composed of the Secretaries of War and State, scientists including Robert Oppenheimer and Enrico Fermi, the Presidents of MIT and Harvard, and others. They unanimously recommended to drop the bomb as soon as possible, and to do so without warning on a major military target to show its devastating strength. It was decided that the psychological blow of using the bomb on Japan would likely bring an end to the war. This judgment was borne out after Nagasaki when Emperor Hirohito's rationale for ending the war was that the Japanese military had not been defeated; a new scientific weapon had changed warfare, and while Japan had to "endure the unendurable," Japanese honor remained intact.

HARRY S. TRUMAN
INDEPENDENCE, MISSOURI

November 29, 1957

PERSONAL

Dear Mr. Cousins:

In reply to your letter of the 25th, I can only refer you to the section of my Memoirs dealing with the use of the atomic bomb against the Japanese.

The main objective was to stop the war. We had tried to convince the Japanese that we had a weapon that might destroy them completely, although we could not explain what it was. Negotiations were carried on between the Japanese and the Allies through Sweden and Switzerland. Unfortunately, the Japanese refused to consider our proposal for surrender, and the bomb was dropped.

I have been informed reliably that a quarter of a million Japanese lives and the same number of American and Allied lives were saved by this action. Three times that many were spared injuries serious enough to cause hospitalization.

Japan surrendered, and Russia came into the war.

I sincerely hope that you will look very carefully into all of these details. It is vital information as far as history is concerned, and many of our so-called historians are not following the facts.

Yours very truly,

Harry Truman

Mr. Norman Cousins, Editor
The Saturday Review
25 West 45th Street
New York 36, N. Y.

President Harry S. Truman, typewritten and signed letter, November 19, 1957.

Truman was explicit in late July in warning the Japanese of total destruction and the urgency to bring the war to an end. On July 28 Radio Tokyo said that Japan would continue to fight, so the atomic bomb schedule continued as rapidly as possible.

Truman wrote in his *Memoirs,* referenced in this letter, "I had realized, of course, that an atomic bomb explosion would inflict damage and casualties beyond imagination. . . . The final decision of where and when to use the atomic bomb was up to me. Let there be no mistake about it. I regarded the bomb as a military weapon and never had any doubt that it should be used."

The atomic bomb not only saved hundreds of thousands of American lives, it also saved millions of Japanese. In June 1945, the government had adopted the *Ketsu-Go* Plan for the stalemate of the expected American invasion. The goal was to inflict losses so severe that the Americans would agree to a peace treaty that would leave Japan with its conquests in China and South East Asia. The *Ketsu-Go* Plan's details were known to the Americans through the decryptions of Japanese messages. A major government minister stated that the loss of 20,000,000 Japanese civilians in the invasion was likely and acceptable; others thought that every Japanese civilian should die fighting with bamboo spears.

The mushroom cloud over Hiroshima, photographed from the *Enola Gay*.

The cloud over Nagasaki.

Truman Proclamation

BY THE PRESIDENT OF THE UNITED STATES OF AMERICA

A Proclamation

THE ALLIED ARMIES, THROUGH SACRIFICE AND DEVOTION AND WITH GOD'S HELP, HAVE WRUNG FROM GERMANY A FINAL AND UNCONDITIONAL SURRENDER.

The western world has been freed of the evil forces which for five years and longer have imprisoned the bodies and broken the lives of millions upon millions of free-born men. They have violated their churches, destroyed their homes, corrupted their children, and murdered their loved ones. Our Armies of Liberation have restored freedom to these suffering peoples, whose spirit and will the oppressors could never enslave.

Much remains to be done. The victory won in the West must now be won in the East. The whole world must be cleansed of the evil from which half the world has been freed. United, the peace-loving nations have demonstrated in the West that their arms are stronger by far than the might of the dictators or the tyranny of military cliques that once called us soft and weak.

The power of our peoples to defend themselves against all enemies will be proved in the Pacific war as it has been proved in Europe.

For the triumph of spirit and of arms which we have won, and for its promise to the peoples everywhere who join us in the love of freedom, it is fitting that we, as a nation, give thanks to Almighty God, Who has strengthened us and given us the victory.

Now, therefore, I, Harry S. Truman, President of the United States of America, do hereby appoint Sunday, May 13, 1945, to be a day of prayer.

I call upon the people of the United States, whatever their faith, to unite in offering joyful thanks to God for the victory we have won and to pray that He will support us to the end of our present struggle and guide us into the ways of peace.

I also call upon my countrymen to dedicate this day of prayer to the memory of those who have given their lives to make possible our victory.

In witness whereof, I have hereunto set my hand and caused the seal of the United States of America to be affixed.

Washington, D.C., May 8, 1945

Kenneth W. Rendell has been a dealer since 1959 in historical letters and documents dating from the Renaissance to the present time. His business, with offices in Boston and a gallery in New York City, encompasses politics, the law, art, literature, music, science, the military, and other areas. He has authored the standard reference books in the field, including *History Comes to Life*.

Forgeries and journalistic hoaxes are among Rendell's many interests. He debunked the infamous "Hitler diaries" on behalf of *Newsweek Magazine* in 1983, and then headed the investigation for *Stern Magazine* into how the hoax had been perpetrated. For Time Warner he proved the diary of Jack the Ripper was a hoax, and he has been involved in every major forgery case in recent decades. He is the author of *Forging History*, the standard reference on the subject.

Another of the author's historical interests is the American frontier. The foundation of his book *The Great American West: Pursuing the American Dream* is his extensive collection of Western American memorabilia; the *New York Times* has said that Rendell's collection "succeeds in giving a sense of the struggle to tame the gorgeous wilderness that stretched beyond the tidy civilizations of the east. . . . It's worth spending time with."

As an expert witness Rendell has offered his testimony in criminal trials including that of the Mormon "white salamander" murders. He received the Justice Department's Distinguished Service Award for his work leading to convictions for thefts from the National Archives and the Library of Congress.

Rendell is the founder and director of the Museum of World War II, which has been described as having no equal (see page viii; website www.MuseumofWorldWarII.org). The museum has loaned major exhibitions and important artifacts and documents to many other museums, including the National Archives, the West Point Museum, the Museum of Our National Heritage (Lexington, MA), the National D-Day Museum (New Orleans), the John F. Kennedy Library, the Newsmuseum (Washington, DC), the University of Southern California, the Imperial War Museum (London), the Harvard University Science Museum, the Franklin D. Roosevelt Library (Hyde Park, NY), the Churchill Museum (London), the Holocaust Museum (New York, NY), the CIA Museum (Langley Headquarters), the Berlin Historical Museum, the Morgan Library and Museum (New York, NY), the International Spy Museum (Washington), the New York Historical Society, and many others. The museum has been the subject of a PBS documentary (narrated by Dan Akroyd).

Rendell also authored *With Weapons and Wits: Psychological Warfare in World War II*. His best-selling book *World War II: Saving the Reality* has won praise from historians and the American public.

Image Credits

All documents pictured in this book are from the Museum of World War II (www.MuseumofWorldWarII.org).

Photographs are from multiple sources, as follows. Front cover, counterclockwise from top left: bpk, Berlin / Heinrich Hoffmann / Art Resource, NY; Getty Images; Library of Congress; Imperial War Museums. Page 4, bpk, Berlin / Heinrich Hoffmann / Art Resource, NY; p. 6, Library of Congress; p. 9, National Archives and Records Administration; p. 10, German Federal Archives; p. 13, German Federal Archives (both); p. 15, bpk, Berlin / Heinrich Hoffmann / Art Resource, NY; p. 17, German Federal Archives; p. 18–19, Getty Images; p. 21, Imperial War Museums; p. 23, Getty Images; p. 26, Gamma-Keystone via Getty Images; p. 28, National Archives and Records Administration; p. 30, Library of Congress (top left), Mondadori via Getty Images (bottom right); p. 33, U.S. Navy; p. 34, Wikipedia; p. 36, Getty Images; p. 38, Wikipedia; p. 41, Imperial War Museums; p. 44, Imperial War Museums; p. 47, West Point Museum; p. 49, Getty Images; p. 51, Library of Congress; p. 53, German Federal Archives; p. 57, Wikipedia (top), National Diet Library, Japan (bottom); p. 60, U.S. Signal Corps; p. 61, U.S. Army; p. 63, Wikipedia; p. 66, Mondadori via Getty Images; p. 68, Time & Life Pictures / Getty Images; p. 70, U.S. Navy; p. 71, U.S. Army; p. 72, Time & Life Pictures / Getty Images; p. 75, U.S. Army; p. 78, AFP / Getty Images; p. 79, Gamma-Keystone via Getty Images; p. 80, Getty Images; p. 84, U.S. Signal Corps; p. 87, U.S. Army; p. 88, U.S. Army; p. 90, Getty Images; p. 97, Roger Viollet / Getty Images; p. 99, Franklin D. Roosevelt Presidential Library and Museum; p. 101, Museum of World War II; p. 102, U.S. Army; p. 103, Time & Life Pictures / Getty Images; p. 104, U.S. Air Force; p. 105, U.S. Air Force; p. 107, U.S. Navy; p. 114, U.S. Army; p. 114, U.S. Army. Back cover: Wikipedia (first and third images), Library of Congress (second and fourth images).

Photographs used in this book but not specified above are from the Museum of World War II.

Index

Documents are in **boldface**.